Some of the Pastor's Problems

BY

REV. M. V. KELLY, C. S. B.

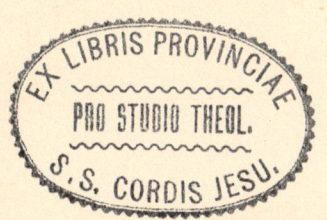

PUBLISHERS:-
ST. MICHAEL'S COLLEGE
TORONTO - - - CANADA

Imprimi potest.
　　　　　FRANCIS FORSTER, C. S. B.
　　　　　　　　　Sup. Gen.

Imprimatur.
　　　　　✝NILUS McNIEL
　　　　　　　　Archiepiscopus Torontonensis

VAIL-BALLOU PRESS, INC.
BINGHAMTON AND NEW YORK

To
Rt. Rev. Alexander MacDonald, D.D.,
Bishop of Hebron,
Whose Devotion to Ecclesiastical Studies,
Untiring Zeal and Saintly Life
Have Been
For many years
The Edification of the Canadian Priesthood,
This Volume
is
Affectionately dedicated by
The Author.

PREFATORY LETTER OF HIS GRACE, THE ARCHBISHOP OF REGINA

Dear Father Kelly:

It has been a pleasure to read the interesting pages you have written and kindly forwarded to me for perusal. Your experience in the sacred ministry has been extensive; you have sought to share the benefit of it with your confreres; God will reward you.

Your desire is to excite zeal for the salvation of souls in the hearts of those chosen by Almighty God to carry on His work of predilection: a great thought and a sublime objective.

How deeply we priests should be convinced that there is nothing more divine than the consecrating of our entire faculties and our every moment to the work on which Jesus Christ lavished His labors, His tears, His time, His Life! How inflamed we should be with longing to have God more and more known, loved and served! How eager we should be to spread the Kingdom of Jesus Christ and to give His Father countless adorers to worship Him *in spirit and in truth!*

No priest can flatter himself that he loves God when he strives not to rescue His living image from the abyss, when he shows no ardor in saving souls, one of whom is dearer to Him than all worlds imaginable; souls destined to pràise Him eternally, to be in heaven the objects of His love; souls He redeemed at such a price.

What an honor for us to have been called to so noble an office! "I would not exchange," exclaimed

PREFATORY LETTER

a holy bishop, "the obligation of working to save souls for the honor of being first of the seraphim. It is better to be an apostle than an angel; and it is a greater privilege to work here at making God known and loved than to repose in heaven in beatific vision."

Then it is our own interest as well that we strive zealously for the salvation of the souls confided to us. Those we do save become just so many mediators to intercede ceaselessly for us in heaven with fervent gratitude for the greatest of all services: and God hears them. Never do we work in vain for God. And if He promises a wondrous reward to the charity which relieves the poor, what will He not give those who have caused His Name to be blessed, His interests to be furthered, who have saved His children from shipwreck and extended His Kingdom over their hearts. If God considers as done to Himself that which we do for the least of His brethren, what will not be the reward and love He reserves for him who, so to say, shall have saved Himself in the person of His brethren?

This zeal to save souls is what you seek in these pages to excite and guide in the hearts and minds of your fellow-priests. God grant that it so animate them to follow His great Highway with calm happiness, that in closing their eyes at the last hour they may tranquilly take their flight to the bosom of their God, there to pronounce the words of our Divine Lord to His Father on leaving this earth: "Opus consummavi, quod dedisti mihi ut faciam" (John XVI)

☩ OLIVER ELZ. MATHIEU
Arch. of Regina

CONTENTS

CHAPTER		PAGE
I	Catechism Teaching	1
II	Is the Parish School Undertaking Too Much?	44
III	Sunday P. M. in Our Churches	56
IV	Parish Societies—Their Struggles	71
V	Can Mixed Marriages be Entirely Done Away With?	91
VI	Instructing Converts	111
VII	The Country Pastor's Weekday	124
VIII	The Country Pastor's Weekday	143
IX	Attending Scattered Missions	151
X	What is the Outlook for the Growth of Catholicity in Our Cities?	167
XI	Catholicity and City Life	184
XII	How Our Clergy are Recruited	195
XIII	Importance of Rural Parishes	200
XIV	Languages in Preparatory Seminaries	211

CHAPTER I

CATECHISM TEACHING

OUR TEXT-BOOKS

ARE we perfectly sure that our text-books in religious instruction are the best possible? No one, of course, disputes the advisability of adopting the best possible. The zeal of our American Catholic people in maintaining schools under a management exclusively religious commands worldwide admiration; how, if within these very schools the best results were not always attainable because of the defective character of the catechism textbooks through the assistance of which that religious instruction is imparted?

In an age when the educational world is ever on the alert to discover methods of assisting the learner to a more ready or more comprehensive grasp of his subject, are we called upon at all to look over the ground again in the hope of being able to lend some additional assistance to our millions of Catholic children, for whom we consider it supremely important that they be thoroughly grounded in the great lessons taught us by Holy Faith? The results of an occasional discussion on the respective merits and defects of Catechisms in use here and abroad, and upon the method of handling them could not surely be other than wholesome. Is it not possible that we fail in this to some extent—that we are not given to examine fully what should be the qualities of an ideal text-book of religious instruction?

The almost universal practice of generations has clung tenaciously to the method of question and answer. Each answer contains a point of doctrine gathered up into one sentence, the words of which no less than the idea beneath it are to be memorized with scrupulous accuracy. Is this the last word on the subject? Or is it possible that future generations may find themselves introducing religious text-books framed on a plan altogether different? Students of pedagogy remind us that there was a time when text-books in several branches of study were written in the form of question and answer. It is one of no less authority than the Professor of Education in the Catholic University at Washington who has something to say on this particular feature of the work. He quotes Dr. McMurry on moral teaching as follows: "Swallow a catechism, reduced to a verbal memory product. Pack away the essence of morals in a few general laws and rules, and have the children learn them. Some day they may understand. What astounding faith in memory cram and dry forms! We can pave such a road through the fields of moral science, but when a child has traveled it, is he a whit better? No such paved road is good for anything. It isn't even comfortable. It has been tried dozens of times in much less important fields of knowledge than morals.

"To begin with abstract moral teaching, or to put faith in it, is to misunderstand children. In morals, as in other forms of knowledge, children are overwhelmingly interested in personal and individual examples, things which have form, color,

CATECHISM TEACHING

action." Dr. Shields adds: "A generation or two ago many branches of knowledge were taught in this way. There were catechisms of history, of grammar and of arithmetic. Even at the present time there exist in our midst schools in which geography is still taught in this manner, and in which language study consists in memorizing rules of grammar and long lists of unfamiliar words, schools in which the children are required to learn by note the rule in arithmetic before working the examples.

"All such procedures result in dead accumulations instead of living growth. These accumulations tend to paralyze the mind of the child and to render it a mere receptacle for words and dead formulæ. All originality and initiative disappear, and the child having dwelt in such a school during the years required by law, leaves it without an enduring interest in any subject taught within its walls.

"Psychology and pedagogy demand a return to the method of teaching which was employed by the Master, who so frequently spoke of the truths which He came into the world to impart to the children of men, but which He refused to announce to those who were not ready to assimilate them and render them functional in their lives and conduct."

Methods of conducting classes have been radically changed in the past half century. All the text-books now used in our parochial schools exemplify the modern method with the one single exception of the catechism.

Is there any particular reason for this exception? Or is it as one has said, "The sacredness which belongs to the ancient doctrines has been unfortunately regarded as attaching also to the antiquated processes of teaching them." There are inspectors of Catholic schools who do not hesitate to say that the text-book of religious instruction in formal question and answer is nothing more or less than a relic of bad pedagogy.

On the other hand we must remember that religious instruction and training are primarily the duty of parents. Christian doctrine text-books must have in view the capacity of those who are to make use of them. It is altogether likely we often lose sight of this. Children attending Catholic schools will learn their religion more or less thoroughly no matter what be the character of the text-book; they have trained teachers to carry on the work. Not so that large element of our population situated beyond the reach of parochial schools, perhaps beyond the reach of a Sunday school. Now, good teaching is largely a matter of good questioning; the professional teacher excels in this; the average parent cannot be expected to possess such qualifications; with him or her it is practically necessary that the text-book supply the questions.

In any case, the catechism in its original form is still with us and likely to remain; to it and to the methods its structure suggests, we may continue to confine our attention.

NECESSITY OF SIMPLER LANGUAGE

Undoubtedly the most objectionable feature in practically every catechism produced for generations in the past has been the use of language and reasoning beyond the interest, if not beyond the comprehension of younger children. We seem to be instinctively prone to run into this error, whether

CATECHISM TEACHING

in speaking or writing of religious things. Many catechisms appear, admirable in many respects, but apparently forgetful of the age and mental calibre of the child for whose instruction they are intended.

The catechism prepared and enjoined by the Third Plenary Council of Baltimore is, in its aim to avoid unintelligible phraseology, a marked improvement on text-books which preceded it. Nevertheless, it is equally certain that the vast majority of teachers using it constantly would welcome an edition whose one distinctive feature consisted in a greater simplicity of language. I recently placed copies of this work before the sixth grade of a parochial school, none of the children present being at all familiar with its contents. The number of instances in which they failed to arrive at the sense was a complete surprise to all witnesses of the experiment. A special test was made with three children proposed by the teacher as being among the very brightest in the class. All three were in their twelfth year, had been confirmed and had spent almost six years in this school conducted by religious. In the list of phrases quoted below there is not one the meaning of which was grasped by all three pupils; to nine of these phrases one or other of the three pupils gave a correct answer. Following is the list:

46. Our nature was corrupted by the sin of our first parents.
    55. Deprives us of spiritual life.
    56. A grievous matter.
    57. The entire answer.
    103. A supernatural gift.
    107. A divine virtue.
    122. The attributes of the church.

SOME PASTOR'S PROBLEMS

124. A doctrine of faith or morals.

129. All its members are in one communion.

134. From whom does the church derive its undying life and infallible authority?

138. Whence have the sacraments the power of giving grace?

146. To attain the end for which He instituted each sacrament.

161. Is baptism of desire or of blood sufficient to produce the effects of baptism of water.

198. Our sorrow . . . should be prompted by the grace of God and excited by motives which spring from faith.

213. The circumstances which change their nature.

236. The superabundant satisfaction of the Blessed Virgin Mary and of the Saints.

287. Laws concerning the civil effects of the marriage contract.

318. By attributing to a creature a perfection which belongs to God alone.

342. Representations and memorials of them.

344. Enliven our devotion by exciting pious affections and desires.

351. According to the nature of the vow and the intention we had in making it.

367. To seek his spiritual and bodily welfare.

395. Mortify our passions and satisfy for our sins.

The reader is possibly going to suggest that very often children cannot do their best in an examination, cannot be expected to explain phrases taken away from the context, etc., etc. I wish to assure him in anticipation that in this case the pupils had the context before their eyes throughout, that un-

CATECHISM TEACHING

limited time was allowed them, that they manifested no embarrassment whatever, and that the only conclusion possible for teacher or examiner was that either the matter or the language was too difficult for children of their years and stage of advancement.

One of the few catechisms which have succeeded in coming down to the intellectual level of their readers is an admirable little treatise entitled "First Steps in Catechism," the work, I understand, of the Rt. Rev. Bishop of Pittsburgh. If my information is correct, it owes its existence chiefly to the author's having found the usual catechisms too difficult for many of the converts he was called upon to instruct. It is worthy of note, therefore, that several books which we have been placing in the hands of young children were found, by actual test, beyond the comprehension of adults in the same walk of life as the fathers and mothers of those very children.

CATECHISM IN THE HOME

If children attending parochial schools find most catechisms too difficult, what will be the fate of children deprived of these advantages? It is really wonderful that the Faith does not suffer greater havoc where such conditions prevail. For assistance the child depends upon his father or mother, or perhaps, some devoted member of the congregation who, without the least qualification for conducting a class, is willing to give her time Sunday after Sunday to any good work proposed. Any one of the three, left to his or her own initiative, might acquaint a young child with many important truths of religion, but usually there is no time for this. There is a specific duty to perform; this is a catechism class. Consequently the method of instruction consists almost solely in obliging the pupils to memorize the words of the book with absolute accuracy. Through a docility of disposition, a sense of obligation, or through compulsion and fear, the child pores over the pages in the desperate struggle to get possession of such sentences as "To serve as an occasion of merit by resisting our corrupt inclinations" or "to be prepared for communion we must be penetrated with a lively faith, animated by a firm hope and inflamed with an ardent charity," or "very often for our correction, to deter us from relapsing into sin, and that we should make some atonement to God's offended justice and goodness." Should he fail, the consequences, he knows, may be serious; and should he succeed, where is the gain? He has learned nothing; he knows no more of his religion than before. He has simply memorized so many phrases and sentences, which, in all probability, he will begin to forget when he is no longer required to be on hand for recitation, often, indeed, very much sooner. The Catholic man or woman who can tell of having recited every answer in the catechism at the age of ten or eleven, understanding only a few of the simpler sections, is found everywhere; they knew their catechism but not their religion.

It is nothing short of marvellous that parents continue to impose such tedious, irksome tasks upon their children without ever seeing or looking for any tangible results, without asking of what benefit is it all. Their obedience in this is blind and little short of heroic. Holy Church, they know, expects parents to have their children instructed in religion,

CATECHISM TEACHING

and so, Sunday after Sunday and year after year, the dull, wearisome drudgery goes on; it is the best they can do; the parents insist in the face of an unceasing reluctance and many unmistakable protests, the children submit very often because no other course is possible. What should have been the most interesting of studies is made a slavery and little accomplished. God, no doubt, rewards immensely the patience and submission of both, and if the most devoted and fervent of all the faithful are to be found among those whose youthful experience was precisely such as I have been trying to describe, it must be due, in the economy of Providence, to their disposition towards the importance of Christian instruction, for it certainly is not due to the efficiency of the instruction in itself. Nevertheless, if we are to believe that the Word of God is the seed which, sown on good ground, will bring forth fruit one hundred fold, we can never cease regretting that all those hours and efforts sacrificed upon the memorization of unintelligible, meaningless formulae were not bestowed upon acquiring an understanding of that word, especially when it was the best of soils that seed might have fallen upon—upon hearts and minds willing to submit generously to the Voice of God, as they were actually submitting to what seemed to them the Voice of His Church.

This is by far the most pleasing side of the picture. There are other children too, not attending Catholic schools, children whose parents are not disposed to adopt such strenuous measures in securing a familiarity with the words of the catechism, perhaps not likely to make any efforts at all, at the same time incompetent to impart religious instruc-

SOME PASTOR'S PROBLEMS

tion unless through the medium of the text-book. Were the task easy, simple, interesting, for both parents and children, something might have been attempted and accomplished; otherwise not. A great deal of the leakage we read of frequently can surely be traced to cases such as these.

We have all these conditions with us now and we shall have them always. There will continue a respectable minority of the faithful to receive little religious instruction outside the home, however much or little it may be their blessing to receive there. Provision must be made for them. Can we not have a catechism in which every question and answer, every phrase and sentence will be intelligible to the average parent, and to the average child of Sunday-school age? Why should we not? Does not every primary text-book in religious instruction fall short of its mission if it does not satisfy this requirement?

Nay, I would go farther and say that a catechism should be a book primarily intended not for the school, but for the home. For, do we not believe and maintain and constantly preach that the work of religious instruction rests primarily with the parent? That the Catholic school is merely an extension of the home, that no religious training in church or school or both, no matter how efficient, can ever make up for the neglect of it in the home? And this is just what systematic provision for religious instruction never does. Whether it be the character of the text-book adopted for general use, or our conception of pastoral activity in relation to this work of zeal, or various discussions, formal or informal, looking to a more effective handling of the matter, it is always the school and conditions

CATECHISM TEACHING

in the school we have in mind, never conditions in, or requirements of the home.

RELIGION A PRACTICAL STUDY

Religion, we will all admit, is a most practical affair; all study of religion is more or less intimately connected with our spiritual and moral conduct. "Not everyone that saith to me, Lord, Lord, shall enter into the kingdom of heaven, but he that doth the will of My Father who is in heaven." In such practical matters as managing a business, housekeeping, playing the piano, who would think of teaching exclusively by word for word repetitions? How favorable would be our comment on the method of an earnest well-meaning mother, convinced that her child could acquire good manners only by learning word for word a text-book on politeness, of which the following would be a sample chapter:

Q. What should be the deportment of children permitted to remain in the drawing-room when visitors are present?

A. The deportment of children permitted to remain in the drawing-room when visitors are present should be reverential, genial, composed, and characterized by a becoming reticence.

Q. What is meant by reverential deportment?

A. By a reverential deportment I mean a conscious and manifested respect for the dignity of those with whom we are permitted to associate.

Q. How can children preserve a genial deportment?

A. Children can preserve a genial deportment by replying to all questions with a pleasant counte-

SOME PASTOR'S PROBLEMS

nance and in a manner free from perturbation and embarrassment.

Q. What do you mean by a composed deportment, etc., etc.?

Now, it is quite true that no mother would adopt this means of instructing her children in social decorum; nevertheless we actually require mothers to subject their children to an ordeal no less trying or ineffective as a preparation for a duty so practical as going to confession. What child should we ever excuse from memorizing word by word the chapter or chapters on the Sacrament of Penance, in which he would find something like this:

Q. What is contrition?

A. Contrition is a sorrow and detestation of sin for having offended God, implying a firm resolution to avoid sin in the future.

Q. What qualities must a true contrition possess?

A. That our contrition may be true it must be interior, supernatural, universal and sovereign.

Q. What do you mean by saying that our contrition should be supernatural?

A. When I say that our contrition should be supernatural, I mean it should be excited by motives which spring from faith and not by merely natural motives.

The ordinary Catholic child has made many confessions—and let us hope fervent confessions—long before he is capable of grasping the sense of a series of questions and answers expressed in such a phraseology. Is it not pertinent to ask, if he has already been trained in the performance of this all-important duty, why insist upon his learning later in life even the very words used by the

CATECHISM TEACHING

author of some text-book to express these doctrines?

There is nothing in life more practical than the sacred duty of making a proper preparation for Holy Communion. To impress the importance of this upon a child and suggest to him means of persevering in it, we require his learning by rote the following:

Q. How should we prepare for Holy Communion?

A. We must be in the state of grace, penetrated with a lively faith, animated with firm hope, and inflamed by an ardent charity. "Penetrated with a lively faith," "animated with a firm hope," "inflamed by an ardent charity" are then severally defined in three questions and answers (to be learned by rote, of course) in language which it is safe to say never yet appealed to any child of any generation, nor had anything whatever to do with his method of preparing himself for Holy Communion.

Artists, poets, literary people in general have left us many beautiful pictures representing a mother teaching her little child to pray. The theme is a favorite one and appeals to all. We all, thank God, know something of the method pursued and, looking back upon it at a distance of many years, recognize that in this the ideal offers nothing more touching than the reality. Yet when we venture to offer assistance in the performance of this duty our contribution consists in obliging that mother to have her child commit accurately this compendium of the doctrine of prayer:

Q. "What conditions are necessary to render our prayers acceptable?

SOME PASTOR'S PROBLEMS

A. We must always offer them with a humble and contrite heart, with fervor and perseverance, with confidence in God's goodness, with resignation to His Will, and in the name of Jesus Christ."

How many children have found the knowledge of this question and answer of any practical assistance?

MEMORIZING WITHOUT UNDERSTANDING

Generally we should be disposed to maintain that a pupil be obliged to learn nothing by rote but what has been thoroughly understood. It is the prevailing practice in the school system of today. Memorizing extracts from literature commences in the very lowest grades and continues a part of the work prescribed when the student is writing for his University Degree. The extracts, however, are always in accordance with the capacity of the learner. Universally admired as is the literary character of Hamlet's soliloquy, who would dream of including it in the memory work of a primary school third or fourth grade? The traditional nursery rhyme, the child's earliest recitation effort, has held its place for centuries through possessing the one single merit of being intelligible; usually it possesses not the first quality of poetry; often it is silly. Readers are prescribed for successive grades of school work in view of the pupils' capacity to understand their contents; only when that quality is assured is there any question of assigning memory tasks. Teachers of geometry a generation or more ago scrupulously insisted on the words of the enunciation being committed to memory; what should have been our opinion of a teacher imposing this

CATECHISM TEACHING

task in utter regardlessness of our having first understood its meaning? The highly commendable practice in colleges and academies of memorizing texts and extracts from Holy Writ supposes the selection of such as the student is interested in. Is all this in conformity with the common practice of catechism classes? Are not our children everywhere obliged to learn catechism answers which they do not understand?

The practice is objectionable, if for no other reason, because of the altogether unnecessary burden it imposes on the pupil. Even if some reasonable justification for the method could be adduced we must realize that the effort to memorize and retain under such circumstances is multiplied almost beyond calculation. In Dr. Butler's Catechism these two questions and answers appear side by side:

(1) Can the bond or tie of marriage be ever broken?

It never can but by the death of the husband or wife.

(2) Why did Christ institute the Sacraments?

For the sanctification of our souls, and to prepare us for a happy and glorious resurrection.

I have never known a child to fail in the former of these answers. I have never known any but the brightest and most persevering pupils to succeed in giving the latter. The reason is obvious; the same results will be discovered wherever the comparison turns upon the intelligibility of the questions or answers.

But at best what is gained? Why should a child be required to expend so much time and energy, not to speak of patience and perseverance, on what to

SOME PASTOR'S PROBLEMS

him is nothing more than a meaningless collection of words? Strange to say the practice has had its defenders even among those whose gravity and intelligence we are bound to respect. Their contention is: "The child will retain the words; later, as his intelligence matures, he will realize the force of them"; surely a most roundabout process of acquiring a truth upon which eternal salvation may depend.

That this method may have any efficacy at all, it is absolutely and primarily essential that when the pupil shall have come to maturer years he still retain accurately what he blindly memorized when a child. Is that very common? Advocates of the system seem to take this as a matter of course, to feel perfectly assured the average catechism learner will not forget. Is their assurance merely a priori, or have they actually put it to a test? If any pastor has taken the trouble to have the young men of his parish,—say between the ages of twenty and twenty-five—pass an examination on the words of the catechism they had in their possession in parochial school days, the report, I have no doubt, would be intensely interesting to your readers. I have not, but I have this other report to make. The majority of a college staff on a certain occasion came forward in loyal defense of Dr. Butler's Catechism, not denying the unintelligible character of the text, but firmly assured of the pupil's capacity to retain them until his developed intelligence evolved their meaning. A few days later it was discovered that, with one honorable exception, the twelve or thirteen teachers taking part in those discussions could repeat only an occasional answer in the words of

CATECHISM TEACHING

Dr. Butler, although this was the catechism all had used in their primary school days. It may be important to add that for years it had been a duty of this honorable exception to prepare the junior classes of the college for first communion and confirmation.

LEARNING BY ROTE

The proposition I wish to make in this issue is so foreign to general usage, undoubtedly most of your readers will not consider it worthy of examination, much less of trial with a view to future acceptance. I dare to maintain that *religious instruction should be carried on with a minimum use of verbal memory.* This, of course, does not apply to learning the ten commandments or anything from Holy Writ.

What is essential for the Christian, primarily and absolutely, is to *understand* the teachings of Holy Faith. Thus far it is purely a case of grasping ideas; in what words those ideas happen to be clothed is altogether immaterial. Because some particular compiler of a catechism happens to have expressed Christian doctrines in certain words and phrases carefully chosen by himself, why must we impose on children the obligation of committing all these words and phrases to memory? Once we are satisfied that the pupil has thoroughly grasped the idea intended to be conveyed should we not consider this enough? Will there be any adequate gain in having him learn scrupulously the formula some one else has used to communicate the idea? If a grammar pupil can readily distinguish

SOME PASTOR'S PROBLEMS

a participle and verbal noun, should the teacher insist upon his learning a set form of words explaining that distinction?

Although almost every catechism in print supposes, by its very structure, a memorizing of the text, although ninety-five per cent of our teachers assume that no other procedure could be tolerated, I cannot remember ever hearing definitely from any source whatever why this method should prevail.

Why should the pupil be required to learn answers by rote? This is certainly the question to be answered. Have any of us ever seen or heard of its being answered satisfactorily? Is it claimed that this is the surest and most expeditious means of *understanding* the doctrine therein expressed? But have we not agreed that nothing should be memorized but what has been first understood? Would any one have us believe that we grasp the sense of a statement not by an exercise of reason or understanding, but by an exercise of memory? Or, in other words, that we understand not by understanding but by remembering what we never understood?

Clearly, if this practice of learning by rote is to be commended at all, it must be entirely for the purpose of retaining. Having got possession of the idea the pupil must next learn by rote the verbal expression of the idea in order to retain it. Now, which is the ordinary pupil more likely to retain—the idea which he has grasped, which he has made his own, which is one of the things he can talk about and put into practice, or the words in which some person else has expressed that idea? In answer to this our ordinary experiences supply endless evidence.

CATECHISM TEACHING

The little child who has been told that there are three persons in God, that Jesus was born in a stable, that He died on the Cross and rose from the dead, that an unbaptized child cannot go to heaven, will remember it all with scarcely an effort, though he has never been required to repeat the words of the catechism in which these truths are stated. The young man of twenty-one, seven or eight years out of school, preserves a clear notion of what is meant by "temptation," "occasion of sin," "grace," "indulgence," of the distinction between "slander" and "detraction," "oath" and "vow," though, if required to pass an examination on the actual words of the catechism, would with difficulty be allowed a report of twenty-five per cent. Or, renew your acquaintance with a young man once tolerably instructed in his religious duties, but for several years neglectful of their practice; he will remember perfectly the importance of a good confession as well as what is necessary to prepare for it, and will have completely forgotten the Confiteor and Act of Contrition.

"But," it will be urged, "surely verbal memory has some place in the work of instruction. No one believes in doing away with it entirely." Certainly not. Pedagogy is a science and this is one of the questions its students have investigated in detail. Would it not be well to bring the results of their inquiries into classes of religious instruction? Is there any reason to suppose that a successful teacher with normal school training must necessarily fail in a catechism class?

The tenets relating to verbal memory in common acceptance among students of pedagogy Prof. Fitch sums up as follows: "When the object is

SOME PASTOR'S PROBLEMS

to have thoughts, reasonings, facts reproduced, seek to have them reproduced in the pupil's own words. Do not set the faculty of mere verbal memory to work. But when the words themselves in which a fact is embodied have some special fitness or beauty of their own, when they represent some scientific datum or central truth, which could not otherwise be so well expressed, then see that the form as well as the substance of the expression is learned by heart."

Adopting this rule in the teaching of catechism, how much of the average class book should we require to be memorized accurately? For the same reason that we learn proverbs by heart, that certain phrases and sentences from Shakespeare are quoted in the humblest homes, we might wisely memorize great religious truths if expressed in language at once concise, pithy and captivating. Bereft of its attractive setting many a proverb the world clings to had, in spite of the great wisdom it treasured, long since been forgotten. Words possessing a charm in themselves we are more likely to retain. And all this is another reason for not trying to memorize the long, verbose, involved, wearisome sentences, the ungainly, uninteresting forms of expression too commonly found in our catechisms.

The prominent educator whose dictum I quoted in the last chapter makes the following rather trenchant pronouncement on the particular method now under discussion: "To insist upon a book of questions and answers being learned accurately by rote is to assume that there is to be no real contact of thought between scholar and master, that all the questions which are to be asked are to take

CATECHISM TEACHING

one particular form, and that they all admit of but one answer. There is no room for inquisitiveness on the part of the learner nor for digression on the part of the teacher, no room for the play of the intelligence of either around the subject in hand; the whole exercise has been devised to convert a study which ought to awaken intelligence, into a miserable mechanical performance, and two people who ought to be in intimate intellectual relations with each other, into a brace of impostors —the one teaching nothing, the other learning nothing, but both acting a part and reciting somebody else's words out of a book." Unsparing as his words appear they not inaptly describe what frequently takes place during the half or three-fourths of an hour the child is obliged to spend in a catechism class.

As evidence of the extent to which the convictions of a great catechist of a previous generation harmonized with the theory of modern educators, allow me to appeal to the saintly Father Furniss, C. SS. R., so often referred to as the apostle of children. In his "Sunday School or Catechism" he gives several pages of specimen questions and answers on different subject, clearly laying it down, however, that "these questions and answers do not suppose any previous learning by heart. They are intend to *suggest ideas* to children rather than *a given form of words to be learned by heart*. A distinct and simple *idea* will remain in a child's mind when a form of words even often repeated will not remain."

The method advocated in this paper—catechism with the minimum of memorizing verbally—had an ardent advocate in the late Rt. Rev. Bishop

SOME PASTOR'S PROBLEMS

Bellord, in whose all too early demise the cause of religious instruction suffered a loss really irreparable. The preface to his admirable catechism boldly announces his plan in the following words:

"This Catechism appeals chiefly to the intelligence of the learner, and not solely, or even primarily, to the merely verbal, mechanical memory. The repetition of long formulas difficult to understand is not knowledge; learning by rote should be secondary, and an occasional aid only to the exercise of the intelligence."

"The chief feature of this Catechism, on which the author principally relies for its success, is that very little of it is intended to be learned by rote, word for word. When children have read a lesson once or twice, or have it read to them, and are then questioned about it, it will be found that they quickly get into the way of attending to sense rather than to words, and of answering more intelligently and accurately than when they are limited to one cut-and-dried set of half-understood formulas. Everything is intended to be, in a broad sense, 'committed to memory'; but the author deprecates the insistence on unimportant verbal minutiae. This only eliminates the attention from that which is more important—the meaning of the truths."

On the other hand, while learning by rote is the well-nigh universal practice, I should like to ask on what authority do we maintain so positively that children must learn their religion in this way? When and by whom was this method decided upon? Or rather was there ever an authoritative decision given to this effect? To all of us who grew up under the system it was represented as an

CATECHISM TEACHING

inviolable tradition. No other system could be tolerated. Very often it has been the sole test. A child who has not memorized the answers given in the catechism is *ipso facto* pronounced delinquent, and will probably be considered unprepared for Confirmation. Thus the practice has obtained so undisputed an ascendency we never think of questioning the legitimacy of its origin.

Personally I am disposed to suspect that the prevailing custom is nothing more or less than a traditional abuse, which has acquired something like a prescriptive right, as the greatest abuses have more than once succeeded in doing.

One consideration is inevitable. This method is precisely what we should have expected of the unskilled teacher, and most of us have spent many an hour learning catechism under the authority of those who meant well and did their best, but who had little experience and less training in the art of pedagogy. It is only the exceptional father or mother who has spent years in the management of a class-room; the young lady with professional experience who will generously give her Sunday afternoons to the Sunday school is still more markedly exceptional. Usually therefore our catechism teachers knew little of teaching. Their devotedness made up for all kinds of deficiencies, but the one fact with which we are here concerned remains —a question and answer text-book in their hands necessarily meant that every answer must be scrupulously learned by rote.

We, as pupils, accepted the method as a matter of course, irksome as its application usually proved. Perhaps relentless insistence upon it, in spite of its irksomeness only served to convince

SOME PASTOR'S PROBLEMS

us of its importance. In any case it was in force everywhere, no less in the Sunday school than in college classes later on. The day eventually came when as junior assistants we were assigned the duty of visiting the parochial school. Here again the same system prevailed. Who were we to assume that all this stern adherence to a practice was totally and radically a mistake? Instinctively, unquestioning, almost unconsciously, we accepted conditions as we found them and vigorously demanded that the words of the book be repeated accurately at any cost. Our successors had had much the same experience and made the same contribution to the support of the system. Thus the tradition has been maintained. Catholic schools, teachers and clergy have clung to this practice not because any council, acumenical, provincial, or local had ever enjoined it, not because names of distinguished educators could be quoted in its support, not because its merits had been substantiated by thorough inquiry or experiment, not because its superiority in results was undisputed, but simply because it had been in possession from time immemorial and we instinctively accept what time and universal adoption seem to have sanctioned.

Another potent influence has been at work helping to perpetuate this notion. Down to the present generation the class-rooms of our colleges attached what is now considered undue importance to verbal recitations as a means of making progress in secular studies. For reasons which need not be dwelt upon here we have been the last to abandon the practice. It is at last gradually disappearing —perhaps has disappeared. If there still remains a teacher of Latin grammar who makes his duty

CATECHISM TEACHING

consist in hearing the pupil recite rules of syntax, quote examples, enumerate exceptions, repeat the "remarks," the "observations," all this with a faithfulness that could not be surpassed in memorizing the Apostles' Creed, and so, day after day, until a hundred or more of such rules, examples, exceptions, remarks, etc., have been accurately committed; if there still remain a teacher of English grammar who insists on all the theory being learned by rote and pays no attention to the exercises supplied by the author, if there be a teacher of geography the walls of whose class-room are never disfigured by maps, it being considered sufficient to require an exact memorization of the words of the book, if there be a teacher whose conception of schoolkeeping is summed up in the instruction, "Go and learn that lesson and then come and say it to me," let us hope such cases enjoy a blissful isolation. Nevertheless this method—or lack of method—obtained not so very long ago. In the work of religious instruction, therefore, should we be surprised to observe a general disposition to fall back on a word-for-word recitation of the Catechism?

A CATECHISM NOT A COMPENDIUM OF THEOLOGY

Authors of catechisms in general seem to experience insuperable difficulty breaking away from the order, the method and even the very terms adopted in standard treatises in theology. Rather they do not break away at all. That such treatises serve their peculiar purpose is not a reason for presuming upon their being suited to the minds of little children. On the contrary, the qualities which especially commend them to students of maturer years and training are precisely such as tend to make their adoption in a junior class an impossibility. The method of exposition by which a primary school teacher and a seminary professor respectively proceed are in most cases diametrically opposite.

Such terms and expressions as "satisfying the Divine Justice," "supernatural gift," "the nature and effects of the Sacraments," "acknowledging God's supreme dominion over us," with which many of our catechisms are replete, are nothing more nor less than the words of theology anglicised. They convey no idea to the child because they have not been translated into the child's language. No work is translated until it is made intelligible to those who are expected to read it. The service the translator renders his fellowmen consists essentially in making intelligible to a large number a literary work which otherwise would have remained unintelligible.

Some critics try to palliate this feature of our catechisms by maintaining that the author addressed himself in these instances not to the pupil but to the teacher. If so, what he produced can hardly be considered a text-book for children; it remains a volume for the use of theologians and scholars, not for those who really need it. He may have succeeded in enunciating the truths of religion in a language accurate, safe and beyond the criticisms of the heresy-hunter, but he has thrown on the parent or teacher the burden of conveying these truths to the young and the illiterate. If the theologian, possessed of some literary skill, will not venture away from the safe moorings of scholastics' technical

CATECHISM TEACHING

terms in order to make an idea intelligible to the young and simple minded, who is going to do it? Is it reasonable to expect the parent or Sunday school teacher to undertake the task?

Not infrequently we hear an elementary catechism commended in the very highest terms simply because it contains so much doctrine in considerably less than a hundred pages. Its statements are made succinctly, with the greatest precision, with grammatical accuracy, with grace and dignity of expression, often with a rhetorical balancing of clauses. Just because all this is achieved the composition is so much the more likely to be beyond the grasp of the youthful reader. Not long ago I heard a worthy pastor make this remark: "I consider that catechism simply marvellous; I knew every word of it by heart before I was ten years old; it was the book we used for years afterwards, but it was only when I had gone over it several times with the children of my parochial school that I realized the wealth of doctrine it contained." What the good father really said was this: "I required five or six years in college, a complete course in philosophy and theology, and several years in the ministry to grasp the full meaning of the questions and answers in that book; therefore the ordinary child should understand them at the age of ten or eleven." The book is probably an admirable compendium of theology, but not a catechism.

A CATECHISM WITHOUT VOCABULARIES

If I am not taxing the reader's attention unduly, I should like to emphasize certain features common to many catechisms which occasion much of the unsatisfactoriness experienced in their use.

That average classes do experience frequent difficulties with the language in which religious truths are expressed, becomes self-evident in the lengthy glossaries considered necessary introductions to every chapter. Are they not at best a necessary evil rather than essential elements of an ideal system? In the first place, they impose upon them the extra task of learning so much more matter by rote. This could be pardoned did the process have the effect of clearing away difficulties. Unfortunately, in many instances, they fall short of the purpose they are intended to serve. To have learned the meaning of a word, or of all the words, in a given passage does not necessarily make that passage intelligible. Countless experiences with Latin and Greek texts in our student days and since have surely convinced us of this.

Instead of drawing up vocabularies why not simplify the language of the catechism? Should that language be not directly intelligible to the child? Should it not be such as to leave no need for vocabularies and explanations? No one can fail to realize the importance of this aim. The question will naturally arise, "Is such a catechism text-book possible?"—another way of asking, "Can the truths of religion be told in language easily understood by the young, the unskilled, the illiterate?" A very grave question certainly, in attempting to answer when one recalls how multitudes of all classes and conditions hung upon the words of Our Blessed Lord. Nor can we suppose it at all likely that the discourses of the Apostles were un-

CATECHISM TEACHING

intelligible to the masses unless provided with a dictionary. God made His revelation for all; is that revelation necessarily so abstruse as to prevent its announcement in terms comprehensible to any but highly developed intellects? To be honest with ourselves and with the world at large, if our catechisms are too difficult for those in whose hands we place them, is it always the doctrine that is at fault? Let us take examples. One catechism in high repute for generations says that "the principal mysteries of religion are most necessary to be explicitly believed"; that "it is a mortal sin to miss Mass on Sundays if the omission be culpable"; that "the church grants indulgences to assist our weakness, to supply our insufficiency in satisfying the Divine justice for our transgressions." Is it not really possible to express these doctrines in language the young and uneducated may follow? Not one child in a thousand will understand the following question and answer taken from the third chapter of a catechism and therefore proposed to the child when he has scarcely completed his eighth year:

Q. What do you infer from the sufferings and death of Christ?

A. The enormity of sin, the hatred God bears to it, and the necessity of satisfying for it.

A vocabulary provided according to custom would offer a definition for "infer," "enormity," "necessity" and "satisfying"; the child would be expected first to memorize these four definitions and then the formal answer to the question. At the end of all this not one child in five would understand the text. Would the work of instruction be

SOME PASTOR'S PROBLEMS

lamentably compromised if the same question and answer were expressed as follows:

Q. What do the sufferings and death of Christ teach us about sin?

A. They teach us:
    (1). How great an evil it is.
    (2). How God must hate it.
    (3). That it leaves a very great debt to be paid.

Again an answer referring to the preparation necessary for confirmation says, "Persons of an age to learn should know the chief mysteries of faith and the duties of a Christian, and be instructed in the nature and effects of this sacrament." The glossary provided defines "mysteries," "duties," "instructed," "effects," and "nature," the latter alone requiring thirteen words. What a memory task for the pupil! Would something like the following not suffice?

Persons of an age to learn should know:
    (1). What every Christian must believe.
    (2). What every Christian should do.
    (3). What confirmation is and what it does for us.

Instances may occur, it is true, when the problem of conveying certain doctrines in simple language and at the same time confining ourselves to the space usually allotted to a question and answer may be beyond us. What does this prove? Perhaps that certain matters in religious instruction should not be written in the form of question and answer; perhaps that a thorough presentation of certain truths calls for a succession of questions and answers; perhaps, therefore, that our present text-books are too small for exposition of doctrine

CATECHISM TEACHING

on this plan. If so, what of it? Where is the objection to enlarging them?

A CATECHISM WITHOUT DEFINITIONS

A priest in an English diocese, for many years prominent in the work of school supervision, among a number of suggestions for the framing of a catechism, asks this rather unexpected question, "Should there be no explanations and fewer definitions?"

The proposal to eliminate definitions entirely, or even to a considerable extent, is one calculated to arouse distrust in the minds of many who will read these pages. More than one will still maintain that catechism should be judged by the number and accuracy of its definitions. The primary school catechisms in common use may be said to fairly bristle with definitions. Every chapter—practically every topic—is ushered in by the invariable "What is—?" The answers are thorough, comprehensive, precise, and usually of considerable length. Not only must the youthful learner be able to repeat an accurate definition of sin; he must likewise have a thoroughly memorized definition of original, actual, mortal, and venial sin. Not only must he have memorized a definition of grace, but also of actual, sanctifying and sacramental grace; not only is his task to define the sacrament of penance, but also examination of conscience, contrition, resolution of amendment, confession, and satisfaction. A text-book lacking all these we should certainly be disposed to consider hopelessly defective. The proposal, therefore, of our clerical friend across the water is so extraordinarily radical as to deserve either the fullest consideration or no consideration at all.

SOME PASTOR'S PROBLEMS

Let us try, however, for the moment to forget the particular form which our religious text-books have always seemed bound to assume, and in the light of our own personal experiences take a calm, unprejudiced view of the alteration suggested. At different dates in our youth we came to understand what was meant by such terms as "Vice, Virtue, Gratitude, Hatred, Pride, Jealousy, Humility and Mortification, of Grace, Blessing, Merit, Indulgence," etc., etc., and we acquired it all without learning a definition of any. Thousands who cannot read use all these words with a correctness not to be required of a catechism pupil. The Catholic laity in general have a conception more or less accurate of what is understood by "Grace." Did anyone actually acquire this knowledge by being told "Grace is a supernatural gift destined by God for our sanctification and to enable us to merit heaven?" Let us hope all practical Catholics understand what dispositions are necessary for a good confession; in this have they received any assistance from being obliged to memorize in youth "Contrition is an interior sorrow and detestation of the sin that we have committed with a firm resolution of sinning no more?"

In our parochial schools of the present day no teacher attempting to give her class an understanding of such terms as "gerund," "adverbial clause," "predicate nominative," "objective compliment," requires the respective definitions thereof to be learned by rote. There is no text-book in print exemplifying such a method. There is not a teacher in the English-speaking world who would dream of publishing such a text-book. The method

CATECHISM TEACHING

is gone and gone forever. Yet many of us are still alive to recall the time when text-books in English grammar proceeded on this very plan just as surely as did the catechisms.

The old method survives in our catechisms most probably because their authors were students of theology—not teachers. Definitions are essential in treatises on theology, or in any work involving scientific inquiry. This is positively no reason for their use in books intended to give young children a knowledge of necessary religious truths.

It is possible that a new departure in this direction is near at hand. Already two catechisms have appeared breaking completely with traditions of the past and attaching little importance to a logical, comprehensive definition. These two works—one from the pen of the late Bishop Bellord, the other by the present Bishop of Victoria—are constantly growing in favor and give every promise of exerting a far-reaching influence upon the future methods of religious instructions.

As substitutes for the use of formal definitions the following may be worthy of examination:

GRACE

Can we get to heaven without God's help?
No.
Can we keep out of sin by just making up our minds to do so?
No.
Who must help us?
God.
How often do we receive help from God?

SOME PASTOR'S PROBLEMS

Constantly.
What is this help called?
Grace.

MERIT

Will all be equal in heaven?
No; "star differs from star in glory."
What can we do on earth to increase our happiness in heaven?
The smallest thing we do in the state of Grace may increase it.
What is it called?
Gaining merit.

DETRACTION

How is a person's reputation injured?
By saying what will make another think ill of him.
If the things said are false?
It is calumny or slander.
If true?
It is detraction.

PERFECT AND IMPERFECT CONTRITION

Why should you be sorry for your sins?
Because they offend God who is so good.
Why else?
Because they caused Our Lord's sufferings.
Suppose you are sorry on your own account, because sin sends the soul to hell. Would that do?
Yes; it is not so good a sorrow, but it will do in confession.
What do you call this sorrow?

CATECHISM TEACHING

Imperfect contrition, or attrition.

What do you call it if you are sorry for God's sake and because you love Him?

Perfect contrition.

AVOIDING ABSTRACT TERMS

The disposition to reproduce the diction of theological treatises, so evident among catechism authors, results necessarily in the use of a preponderating number of abstract terms. In Dr. Butler's Catechism a single question or answer will be found to contain four, five, and in some instances six abstract nouns. In preparing the Baltimore Catechism much was done to remedy this evil, though even there a maximum of six to an answer can be found, while three is by no means uncommon. It would seem as if we had despaired, one and all, of arriving at any other means of expressing our convictions when speaking of the things of God. And, nevertheless, in the diction of Holy Writ how small is the proportion of abstract nouns or of adjectives or adverbs conveying cognate ideas. Some student whose specialty is Scripture study, for example, can tell us definitely if the words "infinity," "infinite," "infinitely" occur even once in the Sacred Text, though when speaking of God, whether in the pulpit or class room, or in print, we seem utterly incapable of getting along without them. Now, since in teaching catechism we are addressing ourselves to a class of people whose every-day vocabulary abounds in the concrete, the text-book to be used should establish a claim to our admiration in presenting a minimum of the abstract.

SOME PASTOR'S PROBLEMS

At what may be considered a sacrifice of dignity and grace of expression I shall venture to suggest the following as possible devices to translate the abstract into something more easy of comprehension:

On account of the disobedience of our first parents we all share in their sin and punishment, as we should have shared in their happiness if they had remained faithful.

If our first parents had not disobeyed God we should be as they were before they sinned; since they disobeyed we are made guilty of their sin and are punished for it as they were.

To make a sin mortal three things are necessary —a grievous matter, a sufficient reflection, and full consent of the will.

A sin is mortal when: (1) a person does something very bad and (2) knows it is very bad and notices what he is doing and (3) is quite willing to do it.

Sacramental grace is a special help which God gives to attain the end for which He instituted each sacrament.

Each sacrament was instituted to help the person receiving it in some particular way; this help is called a sacramental grace.

Persons of an age to learn should know the chief mysteries of faith and duties of a Christian, and be instructed in the nature and effects of this sacrament.

Persons of an age to learn should know:

(1). What every Christian must believe.
(2). What every Christian should do.
(3). What confirmation is, and what it does for us.

CATECHISM TEACHING

Q. From whom does the Church derive its undying life and infallible authority?

A. From the Holy Ghost, the Spirit of Truth, who abides with it forever.

Q. The Church will never come to an end or ever teach anything false; how is it that She has this power?

A. Because the Holy Ghost, the Spirit of Truth, is always with Her.

The Rt. Rev. Bishop of Victoria, the preface to whose catechism announces an effort to present "the teachings of the Christian religion to the little ones in a simple way, after the manner of the Gospel, the concrete being put for the abstract, etc., etc.," offers the following rather novel exposition of a familiar subject.

Q. Can we of ourselves keep the commandments?

A. No; and even if we could that would not save us.

Q. To keep the commandments and be saved, what do we need?

A. The grace of God.

Q. What is grace?

A. The life of God in us.

Q. Can we all have this life?

A. Yes; we must have it or be lost forever.

Q. Can we do anything holy without it?

A. No; our Lord says, "Without Me you can do nothing."

Q. How do we get the help of God?

And again:

Q. What do you mean by grafting?

A. Cutting a branch off of one tree and putting it into another.

SOME PASTOR'S PROBLEMS

Q. Why is this done?
A. So that it may get the sap of a new life.
Q. Is the Christian religion like a fruit tree?
A. Yes; our Lord says, "I am the vine, you are the branches."
Q. What is the sap of this vine?
A. The grace of God.
Q. How is it the sap?
A. It flows from Christ, who is the trunk, into the branches which are the members of His church.

In both the above extracts we have examples of doctrines, among the most abtruse, set forth with surprising clearness and thoroughness, and without the use of one abstract noun.

ONE THING AT A TIME

Barring the pretensions of our modern sociology, there probably is no science in the development of which so many opposing views obtain as in the science of pedagogy. But how widely divergent so ever be the convictions of its several students, all, without a single exception, make profession of faith in the doctrine "One thing at a time" as a fundamental principle. Subjects of instructions so varying in their scope and purpose as algebra, grammar, writing a foreign language, elocution, music, calisthenics, all receive treatment at the hands of skilled and efficient teachers in due subservience to its dictates. The younger the pupils we are striving to advance the greater the necessity of conforming scrupulously to the methods its application suggests. If there is one sphere more than another in which we should feel the importance of keeping this maxim constantly in view,

CATECHISM TEACHING

surely it is in the effort to put the great truths of religion before the minds of little children.

Many of our catechisms, unfortunately, through a desire that every answer be a proposition grammatically, logically and theologically complete in itself, have made the observance of such a system an absolute impossibility, and in many instances proceed by a course almost diametrically opposite. It is another result of looking upon a catechism as merely a compendium of theology, and of failing to recognize the impossibility of presenting truth to beginners by the same psychological processes as prove effectual in dealing with adult minds developed by years of study and intellectual exercise. It is not an argument against this plan that few writers of catechisms have adopted it.

The idea is by no means new even among practical instructors of children whose class experience has been limited almost entirely to the work of religious training. Though written in what now seems the distant past, we find Father Furness, in the work referred to in a previous chapter, maintaining this principle with all the force of settled conviction. In describing his idea of a catechism he declares most emphatically that each question and each answer should contain but one single idea. A statement, definition, explanation, or question which involves a multiplicity of considerations or requires a complexity of phrases or clauses for its expression is beyond the calibre of the youthful mind.

As examples of violating the principle advocated in this paper, allow me to produce here some very familiar quotations.

(a) "No; as the three divine persons are all

SOME PASTOR'S PROBLEMS

but one and the same God, they must be alike in all divine perfections; therefore one cannot be more powerful or more wise than the other."

(b) "Is a person in the way of salvation, who believes in the true church, and says that in his heart he is attached to it, but through pride, human respect, or worldly motives does not make open profession of it or does not comply with its essential duties?"

(c) "That He Himself, directing and assisting by His Holy Spirit the pastors of His church, might teach all ages and nations."

(d) "To recall to our minds, with praise and thanksgiving, the great mysteries of religion; and the virtues and rewards of the saints, and to glorify God on them."

(e) "That the providence of God which often here permits the good to suffer and the wicked to prosper may appear just before all men."

(f) "Venial sin is a slight offense against the law of God in matters of less importance, or in matters of great importance, it is an offense committed without sufficient reflection or full consent of the will."

(g) "The church by means of indulgences remits the temporal punishment due to sin by applying to us the merits of Jesus Christ, and the superabundant satisfaction of the Blessed Virgin Mary and of the saints; which merits and satisfactions are its spiritual treasury."

From catechisms by no means so widely known we quote the following extracts in contrast:

(1) "If a wrong desire comes to our minds is it a sin?

"No, if it is not wilful.

CATECHISM TEACHING

"What is it when it is not wilful?
"A temptation.
"When does it become a sin?
"When we are willing to enjoy it.
"How can we get rid of such a desire?
"By prayer and occupation."

(2) If a person commits a mortal sin can he have it taken off his soul?
Yes.
How?
By going to confession and being sorry for it.
What do we do at confession?
Tell our sins to the priest.
What for?
The priest can take them away.
Who gave him that power?
God.
What sins must we tell?
All our mortal sins.
What about our venial sins?
It is good to tell them, too.

(3) Could you live, work and grow without food?
No; we would soon die.
What is the food of the soul?
Jesus in the Blessed Sacrament.
When did He give His flesh as food?
At the Last Supper, when He took bread, blessed it, and said: "This is My body."
Is the bread changed into His body?
Yes; in Holy Mass.

(4) Who have a chance to get to heaven?
Every one.
What must every one have to be saved?
God's grace.

What makes us sure of that?

His promise.

Suppose we refuse to trust Him notwithstanding His promise.

It would be the sin of despair.

Suppose we expect God to save us when we make no effort ourselves?

It would be the sin of presumption.

It is possible that a catechism drawn up in accordance with the suggestions here and heretofore advanced would turn out a somewhat larger volume than the traditional book of religious instruction, looked upon as of standard dimensions for junior classes. Should this feature constitute an objection? Surely the most serviceable text-book ought to be adopted regardless of size or cost. Could we imagine the author of a text-book in some branch of secular study obliged to abandon a plan of illustrations and exercises merely because its execution would require twenty or thirty pages more than treatises previously in use.

To the objection that the amount of matter in our primary catechisms already overtaxes the memory of many pupils, it may be answered that when there is no longer question of learning every thing by rote, the effort to possess oneself of a book's contents is not necessarily commensurate with the number of pages it contains.

If it is claimed that the price of the catechism should not be allowed to go beyond the time-honored quotation of one nickel, or that the price should be kept down to a minimum, there is ground for questioning the very orthodoxy of the claim. Are Catholic parents to be trained that only the smallest possible fraction of their earnings should be

CATECHISM TEACHING

spent upon the religious instruction of their children? Only a year or two ago the workingman saw the cost of his evening paper arise in one bound from $3 to $6 a year. He proved equal to the emergency. Still we must not think of asking this same man to once a year pay ten cents for a catechism because he had been accustomed to pay only five. The church in America more than any other body on the globe has emphasized the belief that giving in the cause of religion sanctifies the Christian; that our people are better Catholics for being obliged to make rather large contributions to the support of church and pastor. Might we not rather argue that the greater the outlay necessary upon a catechism the greater the blessing upon all concerned. Catholic publishers in order to keep within the limit and, we may presume, reserve a margin of profit for themselves, have turned out catechisms which, in their general make-up, are a disgrace to Catholicity. Is it not about time this should cease?

CHAPTER II

Is The Parish School Undertaking Too Much?

ON one matter we are all agreed—the importance of the home in the Christian education of youth. We recognize that from every point of view parents must be the first and principle teachers. We are willing to look upon the Catholic school as merely the extension of the home; nor do any of us hesitate to assert that the combined efforts of the pastor and religious teachers, the training of church and school, can accomplish very little which will endure when parents have not done their part. At the same time we are all painfully aware that many Catholic homes, particularly in our large cities, are not what they ought to be. What the remedy is going to be, or whether there be any remedy possible, we are not so sure. Our efforts now for many years, in undertaking the particular duties of parents both in church and school, would almost seem to admit the utter hopelessness of finding a remedy in the home. No doubt many a zealous pastor, many devoted religious instructors, have often stopped to ask themselves the question, is it advisable to assume so much immediate responsibility? Are we not taking too much out of the parents' hands? And again the answer came upon reflection, "So many children would be utterly un-

PARISH SCHOOL

instructed in their religion if these practices were not kept up." There is always this terrible possibility confronting us to justify the children's Mass, the arranging for their frequentation of the Sacraments, the occasional assistance at weekday Mass, the teaching of even the Lord's Prayer and the Hail Mary, and the taking over and systematizing of a multitude of duties which are clearly the sacred privilege of parents, and which in previous generations parents, often under circumstances the most unfavorable, attended to well.

The excessive strain of work nowadays imposed upon many pastors and assistants through attention to the parish school, meetings of societies, guilds, social service organizations, arises from the Church undertaking what once was considered the function of the home.

But side by side with the danger of neglect to a certain number of children, which danger we try to forestall by stepping into the breach ourselves, another feature of the case remains for our examination, namely, that *we cannot* take the place of parents—*because God has not qualified us for the task*. One very serious result therefore is that a class of parents who would have done their part admirably well are encouraged to hand over the religious training of their children to us inferior workmen and women. The resultant spiritual loss to those parents as well as to their children is immense. There is hardly any possibility of exaggeration on this point. Parents are sanctified by leading their little ones to God, and our whole system of dealing with children, especially in city parishes with large parish schools, tends to deprive parents of this God-given opportunity. In

SOME PASTOR'S PROBLEMS

dealing with children of the other class of parents, those parents who, we are sure, will neglect their duty, we generally realize in the end that our best efforts have proved little less than a complete failure. A pastor who at the end of twenty years reviews the history of those children who enjoyed all the advantages of church attendance and parish school, but who were without a home training, will find himself face to face with the most discouraging record the sacred ministry can offer. What seemed so full of promise has turned out fruitless. His years of faithful attention, the unceasing solicitude of teachers, a response that teemed with assurances for the future, prospects of completely changing the religious status of the family, all have ended in bitter disappointment. As children they followed the guidance of their teachers, but in a few years they were what their parents had been and continued to be. The contention, not infrequently put forth in reference to certain classes of our Catholic population, that "this generation is gone, but we shall secure the children," has been proved by experience to be a fallacy.

While we are willing to acknowledge that everything depends on the home; that schools, societies, church organizations in general are altogether secondary, we are guilty of the curious anomaly of *expending our best energies on these secondary institutions*. Could not any one pertinently ask us, "If home training is the one great essential, why not concentrate our energies in securing effectiveness there, instead of giving all our attention to schools and societies?" Are we excluded from all supervision of the home? Is our sphere of influence limited to the school-room and the parish-hall? Are

PARISH SCHOOL

we obliged to see that the teacher does his work properly, and at the same time forbidden to influence the parent in the doing of his? Or do we admit our incapability of producing any results in the home? Or do we maintain that there is no practical means of reaching it? Instead of undertaking to fill the place of parents who neglect their duty, would it not be possible to accomplish something in the way of bringing parents to attend to it themselves? What would be the result if some of the time which we give to schools and societies were spent in the individual homes of delinquent parents? If our experience contributes to the effectiveness of the teacher's work in the school, if we are competent to direct the instruction given there, might we not hope to have some suggestions to offer which would enable parents also to do their work as teachers more successfully?

The theory appears sound: is it practical? In attempting an answer, it is interesting to note the information furnished by Cardinal Gasquet in his description of pre-Reformation home. "The clergy had to make sure by personal examination that as children grew up they had been sufficiently instructed in *their religion by their parents*. Should parents fail in this, the god-parents were held to be personally responsible."

Whence therefore the much too common neglect in our day? That some parents are illiterate and uninstructed, in the common acceptance of the term, is no explanation when we remember that among those who have done their part so well there were many who could neither read nor write. Nor were private devotions ever kept up with greater fervor; nor did individual members of the

SOME PASTOR'S PROBLEMS

family commit more prayers, or longer prayers, to memory; nor were one's duties to God and his fellow-man ever realized with greater delicacy than in those homes where, through sheer necessity, the teaching of prayers for daily use and the studying of religious duties had been conducted orally for generations.

But perhaps there are some parents who have never been instructed in their religion orally or otherwise, and who can recite very few, if any, of the prayers which all Christians are expected to know. If so, we pastors have clearly the duty of seeing to it. No matter what provision otherwise be made for the instruction of the children of such parents, we must not forget that those fathers and mothers have also souls to save. There can be no question of our obligation to attend individually, if necessary, to such cases, and we shall do well not to abandon the task until they are both willing and capable of instructing their children. Most parish rectories in our day are well accustomed to the class of adults on one or two evenings a week. It is usually composed of non-Catholics seeking admission to the Fold. Would it not be worth while inquiring whether there are not among our own people adults in even greater need of instruction? Some of these, through a sense of bashfulness, perhaps also through indifference, cannot be induced to attend a class. These however we can generally prevail upon to undergo a course of instruction in private. Such an instruction carried on in the home in presence of the children is sure to produce lasting and most important results.

Some Catholic parents do not realize the duty of instructing their children, because their parents

PARISH SCHOOL

in turn had not realized it nor given them the example. The sooner we can change such a tradition the better surely. If a father in one generation has bequeathed an example of indifference and disregard for the souls of his children, if they recall no instance of his trying to form them in habits of faith and piety, we are doing no small work in providing that these practices be adopted now, with the prospect of their being maintained through future generations.

But most commonly this neglect on the part of parents is due to indifference, irreligion, or dissipation in their own lives, or to an indolence or easiness of disposition which is quite willing that others should assume the burden. To bring such parents to an understanding of their duty, to arouse their energies, to make them reasonably solicitous for the eternal welfare of those committed to their charge, is a task by no means short or easy. Nevertheless if a religious spirit is to be maintained in our Catholic people, if we would hope that God's kingdom be extended among those we have known and worked for, is it not in this direction that our efforts should be turned? If we would labor to make Catholic homes conserve the faith for future generations, where can our energies be more usefully directed than in stimulating fervor and securing a faithful practice of religion in the present guardians of these homes? We may leave the ninety-nine faithful to go after the one that is erring or falling behind. Maybe that one has in his control the eternal interests of a number of innocent children whom he neither knows nor cares how to guide. His ignorance or neglect of duty may seriously imperil the salvation of grandchildren and great-grandchildren innumerable? The means at our disposal to train parents are chiefly the pulpit, the confessional, opportunities of seeing them personally, and the influence we can bring to bear upon them indirectly through the class-room and Sunday school.

1. In the pulpit we should not be satisfied with occasional exhortations on the duties of parents, reminding them of the gravity of their obligations and warning them against the terrible consequences of failing to attend to them. Much of this is in vain when our hearers do not see the application. If criticism be not out of place, it may be suggested that most sermons and pamphlets on the "duties of parents" are altogether too general in character. Parents of the class we are now dealing with need to have those duties explained in detail. They can hardly be expected to teach with the best results, having never had any training by instruction or example to indicate the manner of setting about it. It is a mistake to suppose that most parents know all they are expected to do, and a still greater mistake to suppose they know how to do it. To accomplish all that is necessary in this regard, not only a series of sermons, but frequent series, may be required.

The practice adopted by some pastors of assembling parents on extraordinary occasions for this purpose cannot be too highly commended. Some pastors, to be assured that the more delinquent will not overlook the announcement, go to the extreme of inviting them by personal note. Nor should we allow ourselves to yield to the mistaken tendency of associating mothers only with the obligation of instructing children. Of late years we have all

PARISH SCHOOL

listened to many able discourses prepared for large gatherings of men, such as meetings of the Holy Name Society and the like. Is it not to be regretted that advantage is not sometimes taken of these opportunities to outline to men the personal attention due from them to the religious training of their children?

2. Will a large crowd pressing from without, or even the long wearisome hours, Saturday evening after Saturday evening, excuse the confessor from regularly interrogating such parents as to whether or not they have taught their children their prayers, have morning and evening watched over their faithfulness in saying them, have had them receive the Sacraments regularly and with due preparation, have secured their attentive assistance at Holy Mass.

3. Is there room for controversy on the advisability or practicability of a priest engaging in the rather delicate task of visiting homes with a view to training parents in their duty? What can he do there? He will find fathers who never once in their life have assembled their family for evening prayer. This he can ask for, requiring the father to lead, and most probably discovering that his competency is limited to the recitation of a Pater and an Ave. At once the way is open to commence the instruction of such a father.

If the younger children have never been taught to pray, why not insist upon the parents engaging in this duty then and there? Children who are attending school can be called upon to recite the Catechism lesson, the father or mother being the interrogator. The attention which parents should give their children in their ordinary confessions and

SOME PASTOR'S PROBLEMS

Communions can be pointed out and urged in every possible way. This will also be found an opportune moment to insist on the home being provided with prayer books, Catholic reading matter, religious pictures, articles of devotion, etc. To attempt this work at all is to discover endless opportunities for good, not the least important discovery being, perhaps, the *hopelessness of making any impression on such people from the pulpit.*

Finding time for such visits is the objection which will occur to us. Nevertheless pastors who can devote one evening weekly will before many months be more than satisfied with the results. Will people submit to this? Will they not resent being called upon to give an account of their conduct? The writer wishes modestly to answer from experience and say that no other form of effort which a priest can bestow on the negligent members of his flock will be so thoroughly appreciated as this; in no other way can he so completely gain their confidence; in no other way will he secure a more lasting influence. No Christian with even a spark of Faith surviving will fail to see in this attention of the priest a generous effort for his greatest good.

Will the reader kindly permit a seeming digression? The zealous pastor in trying to bring back the lost sheep is likely to urge the attendance at Mass or perhaps preparation for confession. This is asking too much as a beginning. There is the effect of long, stubborn habits to overcome; there is human respect, and there may be many external difficulties. Moreover, a variety of excuses can be offered as pretexts. Might it not be better to insist for the moment upon nothing more than at-

PARISH SCHOOL

tention to his morning and evening prayers? To this he can positively offer no objection; and if he can be brought to a sincere practice of his religion at home, there is surely every reason to hope that God will soon bring about the rest. The number of Catholics who continue faithful to their religious obligations in private and culpably neglect Mass and the Sacraments is very small indeed.

4. In the regular Catechism classes throughout the year, during preparation for First Communion, and on similar occasions, we can influence parents by constantly imposing upon the children the duty of securing their coöperation, *being careful as far as possible to undertake none of the instruction which the parents are in a position to provide.*

The question naturally arises, How much should we leave to the parents?

(a) Children should never say their morning or evening prayers in school. Some months ago on a visit to one of our cities I noticed that a day college at 8.45 A. M. assembled the students for morning prayer in the church. It seems to me that practice will have two results. In expectation of this exercise the boys will say no morning prayers at home, nor will their parents insist upon it. When their college days are over, so also will be their morning prayers.

(b) From parents, and not from teachers, children should *learn* all the prayers ordinarily made use of in the life of a good Catholic, including prayers before and after meals, prayers upon rising and retiring, the Angelus, etc., etc.

(c) Save in the exceptional, hopeless case, there is positively no reason why the words of the Catechism should be committed to memory through the

SOME PASTOR'S PROBLEMS

teacher's assistance. That is clearly the province of the parent.

(d) No exertion on our part should be spared in having parents accompany children to Mass on Sunday, always allowing of course for the few cases in which circumstances make this impossible. It is they who should be responsible for their conduct and assist them in devoutly following the Holy Sacrifice. This would do away with the children's Mass. It is an institution apparently sanctioned by a usage almost universal. There is much to be said against it, and we are safe in holding that it continues in existence not because it is looked upon as the best, but merely the best possible under certain circumstances.

(e) There was a time when parents were expected to accompany their children when they approached the Sacraments, and the day has not yet come when any of us ceases to admire the practice. Nor should we forget that the conception of this duty entertained by most parents not only guaranteed an immediate preparation and fifteen minutes' thanksgiving, but also exacted of children a spirit of silence and recollection in the hours of Holy Communion, a becoming seriousness in their conduct during the hours which follow, and time for making a formal thanksgiving during several days in succession. None of these can be secured by the Catholic teacher.

In our love for freedom and democracy the principle upon which we all stand is the autonomy, the independence of action in smaller and local institutions. Nothing do we resent more keenly than the encroachments of higher powers. Assumption of what we consider State rights by Federal authority

PARISH SCHOOL

brings every citizen to his feet. Counties and smaller municipalities conduct the affairs which lie within their competence untrammelled by any interference on the part of either State or Federal governments. No one would hear of any of these bodies usurping the prerogative of the three trustees who manage the rural school; who then will feel justified in assuming the divinely-appointed functions of the family and home?

One of our Archbishops, when addressing a Confraternity of Christian Mothers some months ago, used words to the following effect: "While deploring the evils of Socialism, we fail to notice that we are allowing the methods advocated by Socialism to creep into our Church organizations. We all, clergy and people, protest violently against any attempt of the state to encroach on the domain of the home. Meanwhile parents, by forgetting that children are theirs to train and guide, force the Church into an assumption of duties which reduces the Christian family to the status that Socialism would assign to it."

CHAPTER III

Sunday P. M. In Our Churches

WITHOUT doubt our efforts to bring congregations to church a second time on Sunday have been a failure. The thousands who pour in and out of our churches at Mass hour, Sunday after Sunday, are represented by less than hundreds in the evening. This proportion is really above the average. We have all seen large edifices in which Vespers are regularly celebrated with an attendance little beyond the minimum fixed by diocesan statute as indispensable to enjoying the privilege of Benediction.

Differences of conditions give very slight differences in result. If the large city parish, with multitudes to draw from, contends with the obstacle of other attractions in multitude, the smaller city or town, boasting usually of a better proportion, has still to be satisfied with the minority, while the country pastor is forced to realize that the question of distance invariably precludes every hope of accomplishing much in this direction.

Nor is this sparse attendance peculiarly a feature of Catholicity in our own country or continent. The visitor to European capitals and cities of interest will look in vain for overflow congregations afternoon or evening.

This delinquency obtaining everywhere and al-

SUNDAY P. M.

ways and with such persistence has been receiving the attention of many anxious and somewhat discouraged pastors. Various remedies have been suggested and put into execution. From our pulpits we have insisted over and over that the Lord's Day was not sanctified by merely assisting at Mass in the forenoon. A changing of the hour from mid-afternoon to evening, the substitution of various forms of devotion for the liturgical office of the Church, a sermon, a course of sermons, have been adopted as expedients likely to attract people through the interest so furnished. Even with all this we have seen little evidence of improvement. Certainly anyone with something new to recommend in the matter will have an attentive hearing. Any pastor who is assured success in this can be achieved under normal conditions anywhere, and is willing to give the world the benefit of his secret, is within easy reach of a reputation by no means to be despised. There are thousands of us willing to give his plan a fair trial.

The ever-active business world under parallel circumstances would certainly institute an inquiry, with a view of finding out what, if anything, could be done to better prospects. Through the medium of commissions the question would be studied from every angle of incidence; evidence would be gathered, conventions held. Would not their example be worthy of imitation, at least to a degree, amid our difficulties? Has not the time come to give the matter some attention, if not to engage in united effort, at least to discuss causes and remedies, to seek assistance from one another, to profit by the wisdom of those who have had some measure of success? Purely through faith in the efficacy of

SOME PASTOR'S PROBLEMS

such a proceeding, and not at all because there is any past success to record, I dare offer readers some points for consideration.

CAUSES OF DECLINE

In our readiness to admit the fact of declining attendance, perhaps we are too ready to dismiss the subject by a passing allusion to increasing attractions elsewhere, multiplication of motor-cars, and a greater number of business undertakings and social pastimes gradually intruding themselves into the Sunday program of the average citizen. As a matter of fact, certain cities and towns are as quiet and devoid of activity to-day as twenty years ago. That the automobile, because of its capacity for obliterating distance and diminishing the time required to take part in Vespers, should rather promote than interfere with attendance, can be reasonably argued. Then, when we inquire into the movements and habits of hundreds and thousands invariably absent, we actually find there are no special doings or outgoings in their way at all. On the other hand, there are everywhere individuals and families equally confronted with all those possible interferences who nevertheless cannot be charged with delinquency in this. They, like their parents and older members of the family, were doing so twenty or thirty years ago and they do so still. Moreover there are also parishes, not many, it is true, whose churches were filled to the doors Sunday evenings twenty years ago and are not less so to-day. The congregations, as so often happens in large centres, may have changed, almost com-

SUNDAY P. M.

pletely, three or four times within that period; the personnel of administration may have been replaced by another even more frequently; but throughout the same fervor and faithfulness have prevailed. Meanwhile the adjoining parish may happen to be one of those where results suggest the conclusion that the day of second church-going is at an end.

The more attention we pay to the variety of evidence so collected, the more we are likely to conclude that this diminished attendance is less a symptom of some particular turn that the modern religious spirit is taking than of a general decline in that spirit. The replacing attendance at evening devotions by other exercises, private or otherwise, suited to the sanctification of the Sabbath is much less in vogue in our day than a generation ago. Too many people, who still assist at Mass scrupulously and receive the Sacraments with some degree of frequency, look upon further effort as too much, decidedly too much, if it calls for observance regularly Sunday after Sunday. If, therefore, we would continue Vespers or other evening exercise for full churches only, one of two courses seems indispensable: either we must hope to see a large percentage of our people more fervent and proceed to do our part in making them so; or, failing in this, we must tell them plainly that, while they are not expected every Sunday evening, they most assuredly will be looked for one Sunday in four. What is gained by conducting an elaborate service Sunday after Sunday for the benefit of a few faithful ones, who, of the entire congregation, have least need of our attention?

SOME PASTOR'S PROBLEMS

THE OVERCROWDED SUNDAY

Before going further in an examination of this proposal, there is another feature to consider. Are we not all making the mistake of crowding too much—crowding everything in fact—into the Sunday program? A pastor has been busy long hours Saturday afternoon and evening in the confessional and is there again early Sunday morning. With the care of a society, general Communion and other matters of detail that may intrude themselves at any moment, he celebrates a low and a high Mass, and preaches twice, after feeling obliged to emphasize and expatiate on several of the announcements. Many people must consult him on this or that before there is any question of breakfast. Baptisms await him at 2 P. M., and Sunday School is scheduled for the following hour. Three-thirty to four-thirty or five must be given to a Sodality or Confraternity, the success of the meeting depending absolutely on the character of address or instruction he is prepared to give. At seven or seven-thirty, having celebrated Vespers and given another instruction, he would certainly consider himself blessed to be free, it being altogether likely that some parishioner or parishioners (just while they are there and to save a trip down) are waiting to unburden some difficulty. Now, it goes without saying that the physical vigor required to go through these tasks and do each one well is a heritage only one in a thousand can boast of. If any item in the program can be satisfactorily relegated to a week day, it were surely highly commendable to do so.

SUNDAY P. M.

Again, if we confine the public exercises of religion to Sunday, people begin to look upon the religious practice as exclusively a Sunday affair, with the result that they gradually, and perhaps unconsciously, get into the habit of minimizing even private devotions on weekdays. Let us not forget that there are people susceptible of scandal at our policy, admitting to themselves, and sometimes to others as well, that we contrive to get everything off our hands Saturday and Sunday in the hope of being free for the remaining five days. If we would have our people remember the injunction to pray always and give weekdays to God also, it is really important that the influence of the ministers of religion, in some way or other, bear more or less directly upon their daily lives. Our churches are open to them at all hours. We too must do something to help and encourage them if they are to have God before their minds day by day.

RE-ARRANGEMENT OF PROGRAM

To reduce the number of exercises usually assigned to Sunday, where shall we commence? Every Sunday afternoon there are monthly meetings of societies or confraternities. Suppose we make the devotional feature of this monthly meeting consist in attending 7 or 7.30 P. M. Vespers, the sermon thereat being especially intended for the particular society whose turn it is. This arrangement need not necessarily exclude certain other members of the congregation disposed to assist at Vespers regularly. It might be well, however, to insist that all central seats be reserved for members of the society. The church organization which on

SOME PASTOR'S PROBLEMS

such an occasion would fail to secure a generous response for a very large proportion of its enrollment does least harm by becoming extinct. Any society unable to bring out a good attendance one Sunday in the month has little to live for. If our societies are as prosperous as it is in our power to make them, the evening service will edify. A rather low standard, it may be objected. Very true; but much higher than we are witnessing under our present system—or lack of system.

The above suggestion applies to cities and to towns with compact congregations, where the great majority of parishioners are within easy reach of the church. A country pastor will ordinarily secure better results by limiting the number of occasions for Vespers or evening devotions. When such exercises are announced as a special event, demanded by the dignity of the feast, the character of the liturgical season, or a privilege only occasionally provided, a great many will endeavor to be on hand; when they take the form of a routine, a something occurring weekly with no definite objective attached, all but a rare few will ignore them altogether. When the country pastor has two or more churches to attend, he can secure an evening congregation almost every Sunday by judiciously distributing the opportunities among all.

But whether in city or country or town, success will necessarily depend to a great extent on the character of sermon they may expect to hear. When it bears evidence of importance in our own estimation and of special earnestness and care and effort in its preparation, people will instinctively look upon the occasion as worthy of effort on their part. If, on the contrary, we give them reason to suspect

SUNDAY P. M.

that we allowed the hour to approach in the hope of getting through without any special exertion, they are likely to assume that no exertion is expected of them either.

The proposal to hand over the Vesper hour to society meetings may suggest the objection: "What will become of the catechetical instruction for adults enjoined by our Holy Father Pius X?" I very much fear the tendency of the hour suggests the objection: "What *has* become of it?" This legislation was received with worldwide acclaim only seventeen years ago. The hierarchy everywhere, pastors, religious, ecclesiastical publications foresaw in it the most beneficial results. Frankness obliges us to admit we have not made it a success. But the advisability of keeping a place for it among the Sunday exercises rather than relegate it to a weekday has really had nothing to do with the failure. Our inability to make it interesting is the real explanation. All our training and experience had been along lines entirely different. That a preacher spoke readily, fluently, consecutively, eloquently, even forcibly did not establish his capacity to catechize. It was a new field for effort and most of us needed special training in the art. Until our seminaries undertake to drill in pulpit work along the lines contemplated in our Holy Father's encyclical, failure will continue to be the prevailing condition.

OTHER SUNDAY OBSERVANCES

Are we possibly making the further mistake of exhorting our people too urgently on the importance of attending Vespers and Benediction to the

SOME PASTOR'S PROBLEMS

exclusion of other commendable practices? What about a crusade against the Sunday paper? The Catholic who fritters away hours (or large portions of hours) over the pictures and printed matter of a forty, fifty, or sixty-page publication is not likely to set aside another period for the reading of literature of an edifying character. Let us hope that the notion of something in the way of religious reading on Sunday is not yet too old-fashioned for reasonable people to entertain. Even if our pulpit utterances rarely touch the subject, there are, at least, two things we can accomplish—first, forbid the Sunday paper admission to our own quarters; secondly, forbid the newsboy offering his wares at the church door.

Again, the number of Catholics who systematically arrange or offer themselves to take part in one or other spiritual or corporal work of mercy as a means of sanctifying Sunday is shamefully small. Is not the fault to a great extent ours? From coast to coast how many of our pulpits are accustomed to regularly outline undertakings of this sort and propose them as Sunday afternoon occupations *for all?* Even when we zealously instruct our people on the necessity of something more than assistance at Holy Mass on Sunday, somehow or other we seem to lay undue emphasis on such exercises and activities as we ourselves are personally and primarily taking part in. There is no congregation whose members may not find many opportunities of doing a kindness. People neglected and forgotten are everywhere. Some are suffering in hospitals with no friend within reach; invalids who see only the same faces and live amid

SUNDAY P. M.

the same scenes week after week, year after year; old people left very much to themselves because the time to make new friends has gone; poor, struggling families who watch the more fortunate go by unheeding, perhaps despising, their miserable state; the lowly and forgotten who would be cheered by even a few moments' recognition; the dissipated and reckless for whom a little consideration is often encouragement sufficient to attempt a reform—but the list is endless. How many of our people who inquire about places of recreation to visit on Sunday afternoon might, under pressure of repeated reminders and exhortations, come to realize that there are important duties they had all along been neglecting? It may be safely asserted that the more works of mercy and zeal a congregation engage in as part of the Sunday program, the greater proportion will turn out on an occasion of public devotion. And this brings us back to where we started—that people fail to attend Vespers chiefly because they do not fully realize the obligation of sanctifying the Sabbath. The sacredness of Sunday is being forgotten. Our people must be asked to remember that this is the third of God's Commandments, upon the observance of which so largely depends the preservation of faith and reverence for sacred things, enjoined by the first and second respectively. It is God's positive law defining and enjoining a necessary means to the observance of those fundamental duties toward Himself. It is significant that in continental cities, wherever Sunday P. M. came to be considered as essentially a time for recreation and distraction, irreverence first, and then loss of faith, invariably followed.

SOME PASTOR'S PROBLEMS

THE MOST EFFECTIVE INSTRUMENT

If, then, among those around us good old practices are passing away, it behooves us to stand at the helm, to once more tighten our grip and struggle vigorously to bring things back to where our staunch and faithful forebears left them. We shall accomplish little without having recourse to the advantages we possess in the sacred tribunal. Very likely we shall find few penitents concerned about delinquencies of this sort, provided they contrive to get to Mass Sunday morning. One is tempted to ask how great has been the endeavor to dispose of large crowds of penitents within a limited time, with the consequent conviction that it is impossible to consider anything beyond what is absolutely essential; the almost feverish haste with which one after another is admitted and dismissed being responsible for the people's failing to appreciate the importance of spending the Sabbath better. When confessors will insist on having time to instruct where necessary, to exhort earnestly and fully, to point out duties overlooked, are we likely to find the faithful looking upon the hours after Mass solely as glorious opportunities for worldly pastime and distraction?

Theology tells us a good deal about remedial penances. What would be the effect, if, for the eternally enjoined litany, or rosary decade, or five Paters and Aves, we should substitute assistance at Vespers, a half-hour of religious reading, an occasional Sunday P. M. call at the indigent ward of the hospital, a few moments with the neglected, aged, or invalided, or the condescension required to while

SUNDAY P. M.

away a small part of one's leisure hours trying to give some encouragement to the unfortunate struggling poor?

IS THE SUNDAY SCHOOL WORTH WHILE?

I once heard a respectable pastor remark: "We got the Sunday School from the Protestants; in any case it is no use." This rather scathing criticism of a universally adopted institution some of us may be slow to sympathize with. It has been given a fixed place in our Sunday afternoon program. Are results at all in keeping with the time and attention it claims? As a means of providing for the religious instruction of young children does anyone point definitely to the great good it accomplishes, or regard its possible discontinuance a calamity?

There are many things to consider.

1. Almost every priest in charge of souls has more leisure for this duty on weekdays than on Sundays.

2. In almost every parish, no matter how varied the circumstances, children can be more conveniently assembled on weekdays.

3. With only a few exceptions, lay people who can be secured to conduct Sunday-school classes are not capable of anything effective. Their principal service consists in having children recite the words of the text-book, a task in which much better results can be secured by the parents. Young men and women who have spent years in Catholic colleges or academies, and are therefore to a degree presumably qualified, are usually the most unwilling to take part in such work. Professional teachers, as a rule, claim exemption on the plea that the strain of

SOME PASTOR'S PROBLEMS

conducting a class five days weekly entitles them to relief on Sunday.

4. The one parish assured of competent teachers is that in which religious conduct the parish school, and where, consequently, there is least need of it. It can be reasonably contended that religious instruction five times a week for eight or ten years is enough. So convinced are pupils of its sufficiency that they never contemplate preparation for the Sunday-school class, a circumstance which has much to do with the inattention and disorder frequently characterizing procedure there.

5. An argument on the defence maintains that assembling children every Sunday afternoon at least trains them to the habit of sanctifying Sunday. So far so good. But do we actually find that they acquire the habit? When those years are over, do children so trained attend Vespers and Benediction faithfully?

6. But unquestionably the gravest objection to a Sunday school is the depriving parents of the most favorable opportunity afforded them to instruct their own children Two trips to church will generally be considered a full day. Certainly we must insist that children be made to realize something more is required than mere assistance at Mass; but why not also try to make parents realize that the obligation is theirs primarily, and suggest practices they must undertake to enforce?

A reply in such terms as "visionary," hopeless," "wasted effort," will not be at all unexpected. Absolute diffidence in the parents' willingness or capacity to assume responsibilities essentially theirs is a widely prevailing sentiment, too frequently evidenced both in word and in practice. Is it really

SUNDAY P. M.

so that we can no longer hope to have them do their part in the religious training of their children? Is it not possible that their undoubted negligence is largely due to our usurping their functions?

A NOVEL EXPERIMENT

It is yet, unfortunately, too soon to report on an experiment which one pastor declares he is determined to see to a finish. On Sunday at 2 P. M. the church bell is tolled; its tones can easily be distinguished beyond the farthest limits of the parish. All understand it is a signal for an hour's religious exercise in every home. Children are to take up their catechisms, parents to help them with it; other adult members of the household to occupy themselves in some way suitable to the occasion, singing hymns, reading religious books or even the Catholic weekly paper being among the occupations recommended. Neighbors and acquaintances disposed to make a call understand that sociabilities commence only at 3 P. M. Precisely at 2 P. M. also the pastor's auto is backing out of the garage. He finds time to drop into at least three or four houses—no one being able to guess which three or four will be favored. He conducts a short catechism class in one, suggests reading matter in another, and so on. Already he has reason to hope that the number of houses in which eventually it will be important to call can be reduced to an easily manageable few, a great majority of the people showing the highest appreciation of the scheme and being quite pleased to second his efforts. For the sake of giving a little variety and interest to the plan, occasionally at the end of about five or six weeks perhaps, an assem-

SOME PASTOR'S PROBLEMS

bling of all the children in the church is announced. Of course, the religious instruction of children is by no means confined to these efforts, the essential purpose being to throw the responsibility of the proper Sunday observance upon the guardians of the home. Let us hope the experiment will not be a failure.

CHAPTER IV

Parish Societies—Their Struggles

OF church societies there is no end. As to their effectiveness there is both difference of opinion and difference of result. There are few of us who have not known parish organizations here or there accomplishing wonderful things in the cause of souls. There are still fewer who have not been face to face with sodalities and confraternities dragging out a miserable existence and instrumental for good chiefly in the reward a few faithful members deserve for burdens imposed upon them. There is in all this, however, no cause for discouragement. The matter is entirely in our own hands. There are everywhere possibilities for a successful society, and we all understand that a parish society is what the priest in charge makes it. Without this energy it may live, but it cannot prosper. Its prosperity is usually in keeping with the degree of interest and attention he bestows upon it. Probably the only exception is the Knights of Columbus. For whatsoever reason, that body has a power of development in its own inherent vitality.

Unfortunately, the ordinary priest, whether pastor, or assistant, has imposed on him a duty of managing a society, or societies, without ever having been told how. Is there not something neglected here? Is there not such a thing as showing the be-

SOME PASTOR'S PROBLEMS

ginner what line of procedure to adopt, and suggesting activities which tend to stimulate interest and produce results in the right direction? The means of securing that success, which some pastors have arrived at only through years of intelligent effort and experience, could surely be explained to the beginner. As our primary schools are conducted to-day, very few, if any, of our most capable young people could carry a class through its prescribed program of studies without a training in pedagogy; at least ninety per cent of those who pass a year in a normal school, though many of them possess very ordinary attainments otherwise, do this work well. There is scarcely a business position for which a young man is considered qualified without a thorough schooling in methods and details. Salesmen, travellers, insurance agents, book canvassers, promoters—all must be taught their lessons. Most of us would be astonished to hear of the number of night schools in larger cities whose purpose is to give instruction of this nature. Not the least part of this form of endeavor is the system of training the raw recruit how to meet and handle men. Conventions of one form of business or another are held regularly throughout the country with the same object in view. Could not the young priest also in this, the most practical, if not the most difficult, of his duties receive some help from the experience of those who have gone before and won success?

Hitherto in our seminaries the program of work has made little provision for this line of training, and works on Pastoral Theology, admirable beyond question in all they undertake, in the treatment of work among parish societies are disposed to exhort rather than suggest or direct.

PARISH SOCIETIES

It is not surprising, then, that some priests spend little or no effort on the work, not knowing what to do nor realizing how anything could come of the effort; that others try and to a great extent fail, but through a sense of duty or of loyalty to institutions established with the highest ecclesiastical approbation, struggle on in the dark, either to find a means of controlling the situation or eventually to give up in despair. Others, professedly believing that little is to be gained from confraternities, offer no objection to those they find in existence and allow them to work out their own salvation or destruction.

Nevertheless we must agree that an interest in the work can be cultivated, an interest sufficient to arouse activity and insure good results; moreover, that the lack of both interest and energy in this, as in everything else, is mainly due to want of confidence in our own ability to cope with the difficulties arising. With the hope, therefore, of promoting further discussion of the subject, I venture to offer a few suggestions which have come to me in the direction of parish societies during a fairly long and varied experience in the ministry.

Organizations existing in most large parishes may be divided into two classes. First, there are those established to carry on a specific work of zeal; among these are the Confraternity of Christian Doctrine, Altar Societies, the St. Vincent de Paul Society. Then there is the class of societies whose chief purpose is the sanctification of their respective members by the observance of certain rules, the advantages of special instruction, mutual good example, and certain devotional practices. With the latter in particular this essay is concerned.

SOME PASTOR'S PROBLEMS

Not many will object to the principle that the number of societies should be limited. Societies in unrestricted numbers are mutually destructive. Your ordinary parishioner, man or woman, is doing well if he complies strictly with the requirements of one. Any society is better dead and unheard of than existing and unprosperous. A society with only a small proportion of faithful members defeats its very purpose, for instead of encouraging one another the members become a mutual source of disedification. From this point of view four will be found to suffice: one each for men, boys, young ladies, and married women, respectively.

THE MEN

No other church organization in our day has done, or is doing, so much to promote among men frequentation of the Sacraments as the Holy Name Society. Whatever the explanation, there is undoubtedly something, either in its origin or purpose, which especially appeals to men. That non-Catholics and the public press generally are everywhere ready to express a generous admiration for any strictly Catholic organization is, to say the least, significant. The day is probably at hand when practically every parish in the land will have its branch of this salutary Society.

Whether general Communions should be monthly or quarterly depends entirely on the other question—"What object does the pastor wish to further?" Is it frequent Communion for a large number of men already well disposed, or regular Communion for all? By vigorous efforts on the part of the pastor or director a fairly large proportion will

PARISH SOCIETIES

turn out monthly, at least for some time. But are these the men about whom we are really solicitous? Would not many of these be exemplary in the frequent reception of the sacraments without any society at all? On the other hand, in nine parishes out of ten there is a very appreciable number for whom quarterly Communion is decidedly frequent. If the influence of the Society does not extend to these, what have we accomplished? Suppose we succeed in having all do this much, may we not trust that the more fervent members, through other influences at our disposal—the pulpit, the confessional, the celebration of feasts—will easily be brought to more frequent attendance at Holy Communion? Almost any man, however indifferent or uninstructed, dislikes being counted out altogether. He will make some effort to be with the crowd. Example, above all, has weight with him; he can entertain the idea of taking part every three months, but not much oftener. As director of a branch in which quarterly Communion was the rule my personal experience has been that every occasion of general Communion in a term of eight years brought delinquents to the sacred tribunal. By "delinquents" I mean men who had neglected their Easter duty for periods of less or greater duration. It is certainly worthy of note that more than once a quarterly Communion of the Holy Name Society saw more delinquents approach the railing than was the result of a week's mission for men exclusively conducted toward the close of these same eight years.

Similar reasons exist for the quarterly meeting. Few men will attend monthly meetings regularly from pure devotion; not many will attend once a

SOME PASTOR'S PROBLEMS

month, even when the meeting is made a social affair. So many have to give evenings to fraternal societies, trade or labor organizations, athletic clubs, etc., etc., not to speak of the theatre and the thousand forms of amusement, that we cannot expect them often. The greatest inherent force a society possesses is full attendance, whether at meetings or general Communions. The member who witnesses that will almost certainly come back the next time; we must labor to secure it at any cost. When we can arrange for a meeting on the Sunday afternoon or at some other date immediately preceding the quarterly Communion, one helps to announce the other and serves to concentrate interest on the occasion. It is altogether advisable to appoint a number of promoters or prefects of districts whose duty it will be to call personally on each member within his precinct a few days previous to the quarterly meeting. Every prefect should be made to feel that his absence from a meeting or general Communion thereby disqualifies him for the position. By assigning certain pews to each district on the morning of general Communion we shall enable prefects to keep an exact record of the attendance of their members for the year. Strict attention on the part of prefects to these details, coupled with vigorous announcements from the pulpit, will not suffice to bring out every man faithfully even four times a year; we shall be surprised to learn how many can ignore the appeal. The best results cannot be obtained short of a personal visit from the pastor or one of his assistants. Apart entirely from the special interests of the Holy Name Society, it is not too much that the more or less responsive class enjoy the visit of a priest four times a year.

PARISH SOCIETIES

If, during the week immediately preceding the quarterly Communion, priests of the parish can arrange to give the hours after 5 or 5.30 P. M. to calling upon the men, married and single, and especially upon those of whom they see the least, the success of the Holy Name Society is practically assured.

When meetings come only at the end of three months it will not be difficult to provide a program, interesting and attractive. A member should feel that there is something worth going to. Whether it consists of a special sermon with Benediction of the Blessed Sacrament, a lecture by some priest or Catholic layman, a discussion bearing on the work of the society, or, as is advisable now and then, a literary or musical entertainment, neither trouble nor expense should be spared to prevent the time being occupied with what will merely seem a dull and meaningless routine. See that the meetings are lively and the occasions of receiving the Sacraments devotional and orderly. Provide confessors numerous enough not to keep the men waiting; exclude women from the confessionals on those Saturday evenings, and thus let the men understand that the occasion is theirs and that their presence is expected. Give the society precedence at the Communion rail on Sunday morning; prepare a short discourse suitable to the occasion; have them supply congregational singing—a hymn or two; require them to give suitable time to thanksgiving, the director remaining in their midst during the entire ceremony.

The regulation providing that upon the death of a member a number of Masses—twenty or thirty—be offered for the repose of his soul, appeals warmly to all and has a rare force in maintaining interest in the society. Directors will do well to look after

SOME PASTOR'S PROBLEMS

this with scrupulous attention and refer to it regularly when addressing meetings or speaking of the Society from the pulpit. *The Holy Name Journal* strongly recommends assuming charge of certain parish activities with a view to imparting interest in something over and above the prescribed devotional practices. The manner of carrying out this suggestion will necessarily vary with the conditions obtaining in particular parishes. It is always important, however, that work undertaken with this object be such as to command the interest and invite the coöperation of all the members.

Certain dioceses have a central executive committee, which is really necessary to arrange for annual processions and for other undertakings that several branches unite to carry out. Like all central administrations to which a federation of local organizations gives rise, its tendency is to usurp functions strictly within the competence of the individual body. Herein is a serious danger. Each branch must be jealous of its autonomy and insist upon exercising full control over all its doings within the parish, and over such movements as are carried through by the local organization without the assistance of other branches. The more any branch asserts its independence in managing its own affairs, the greater service it will render itself and the Holy Name Society as a diocesan body. The qualification for rendering valuable service is vigorous life in the individual called upon for service.

THE BOYS

A junior Holy Name Society for boys under eighteen years of age is much easier to conduct.

PARISH SOCIETIES

Generally it is wise to keep the age of admission well advanced. The line may safely be drawn about twelve, or better perhaps, at the reception of Confirmation. The younger boys will look ahead ambitiously to this promotion, while it is instinctive with those of sixteen or seventeen to resent being associated in any way with children of lower grades. Of course, monthly Communion must always be the standard here. Universal conformity to this can be secured, though it will probably be found necessary to keep an exact record of attendance on each occasion and to insist that every case of absence be accounted for. Any system for carrying this out will very soon give adequate results. I know of no means at once so simple and so effectual as that of immediately notifying the parents of the absent member and requesting them to have him make up for the delinquency within a day or two. Filling in the blanks on a printed postal card conveying this message and bearing the signature of the Reverend Director is the work of only a few seconds and invariably insures amendment next month. The parent is rare indeed who fails to appreciate this evidence of a pastor's or assistant's interest in his or her boy, and in the boys generally. The effects may often be far-reaching, even beyond all expectations, and there is not the slightest danger of most sensitive parents resenting this plain intimation of neglected duty on their part. An occasional friendly remark will make the older boys understand how much depends on their example. Should the boys of seventeen take the liberty of excusing themselves from regular attendance, the boys of sixteen will soon claim the same privilege.

If a religious society has one purpose more than

SOME PASTOR'S PROBLEMS

another, it is surely that of inspiring the greatest reverence for the Sacraments and teaching its members to receive them not only regularly but also with all possible devotion. Accordingly, as a training for the future, as well as to insure a fitting preparation for Holy Communion, insist that all who are free to do so, go to confession on Saturday. The boys who work Saturday afternoon and evening should have the fullest assurance of an opportunity to go to confession Sunday morning. On those Sunday mornings a priest is quite justified in asking all other penitents to relinquish their place near the confessional in favor of boys who have been at work Saturday afternoon and evening.

The Reverend Director, who should remain with them during Mass, will reserve a number of pews for their use, preferably near the altar, and will have them take their places in an orderly manner, wearing badges, and never without a prayer book. It is much better to see that each boy read his own book attentively than to fill up that hour with certain devotions made in common, such as reciting the beads, singing hymns, or repeating certain prayers in concert. We are all so much creatures of habit that in this formative stage the method of assisting at Mass and making thanksgiving after Communion should be just that which they can always practice with greatest benefit in after life. The boys' society, and for that matter all societies, should have precedence in going to the railing on their respective days of general Communion. In churches where giving Communion takes up from ten to twenty minutes this regulation means a great deal, and members who are faithful to the society will be encouraged by this mark of favor.

PARISH SOCIETIES

A more lively attachment to the society can be maintained where it is possible to conduct an athletic organization in connection with it. A club room, reading matter, debates, etc., mean little to the majority of boys under eighteen, and something in common, outside the religious exercises, is very desirable. Failing everything else, the director can get them together on special occasions; it is altogether advisable to have them take part in church processions, entertainments, etc.; an outing now and then is everywhere possible. It is important, of course, that the call upon the society is one in which the members can participate.

THE YOUNG LADIES

It would seem almost heterodox not to associate the name of the Sodality B. V. M. with this portion of the congregation. I am not sure that I have ever understood the exact purpose of this now long widespread institution. In many parishes the qualifications for membership tend to make it select and exclusive. Only those who can promise exemplary strictness of conduct, even to the extent of giving up much of what is sanctioned by custom, is considered eligible. A limited number of young women leading lives truly edifying can thus be guaranteed. The effect upon the entire congregation must be wholesome. A higher standard of piety is put forward; frequentation of the Sacraments is encouraged; a small body of willing workers is available for certain lines of church work; many little services in the way of decorating the altar can be counted on.

When all is said and done, however, we cannot

help feeling that they who least need looking after are receiving our special attention. Are sodality meetings merely pious occasions filling in an idle hour on Sunday for young women whose strictness of living preserve them from the temptation of spending Sunday afternoons elsewhere? We assist at meetings, prepare sermons for them, busy ourselves with what is going on, all the time realizing that our efforts are in behalf of the devout and well-behaved few, not of the young, or unprotected, or indifferent.

What can we do for the large majority who constitute this latter class? Will the canonically erected Sodality of the Blessed Virgin, with its lofty ideals and fixed rules, admit local modifications such as to throw open its doors to all? And if not, are there not parishes in which some other organization less rigidly constituted might be an instrument of greater good for a greater number? Now that our cities are filled with young women earning a living under ever-varying conditions, away from home, isolated, not under any special religious influences, exposed to dangers more or less threatening, are we not called upon to include them in our schemes for promoting good or fortifying against evil? But this we cannot have, if admission depends upon many pious observances or giving up many practices which society is tolerating. Suppose our chief end be that every young lady in the parish without an exception approach the Sacraments regularly—at least once a month—trusting to other means and influences to promote frequent Communion among those so disposed, how can it be accomplished?

The very first condition of success is probably the

PARISH SOCIETIES

fixing of an age limit. Any priest who has had the direction of a Sodality knows how much the younger portion object to identifying themselves with assemblages or public gatherings in which a considerable number of the more advanced in years are prominent, and it is always this latter class who appear most faithfully when devotional exercises or church work is the object. A line has to be drawn, no matter how delicate the undertaking. I knew a pastor who was accustomed to face the situation with the following announcement: "We require all the girls to attend Sunday school until they are fifteen years of age at least; for the next nine or ten years we shall endeavor to do all we can for them in the Sodality; but after that they must look after themselves the best they can." Thus it was made clear that all single ladies beyond a certain age were not eligible for membership.

If there are some young women in the congregation whose families are possessed of wealth, or enjoy a certain social prestige, their attendance at Sodality meetings must be strenuously insisted upon. A Sodality director has to deal with people keenly sensitive to any evidence of class distinction. There is always a very large number who, having to choose between being absent with the socially recognized or present with the housemaid and factory girl, will soon come to a decision. The consequences to the Sodality are fatal. Membership must be made fashionable. Good Catholic families blessed with some worldly importance can be made to understand this, and should be induced to make good use of the influence God has placed in their control. Under such circumstances it is generally better to look upon the Sodality as a purely religious organization, not imposing obligations of a social nature. There may be several most exemplary at every call and capable of real leadership in church work who jealously claim the privilege of social exclusion. "Not Genuine Christianity"—some one may rejoin. Perhaps so, but why feel obliged to attempt the impossible?

When the aim is to assemble all, one meeting in the month will be found sufficient. This supposes a strict insistence on full attendance and pains being taken to make the occasion worth while. When a sermon carefully selected, carefully prepared, interesting, adapted to the audience, may be expected, there is little difficulty in securing a generous response. We are often heard deploring the decline of religious sentiment, perhaps of true womanly character, among the young ladies of our day. We know how many have received but limited instruction, how many are left almost entirely without guidance, what room there is for enlightenment among the so-called better classes; and no priest in charge of souls can feel guiltless should he fail to make the most of an opportunity such as is afforded by a well attended Sodality meeting. Their choice of company, their reading, pleasure-seeking, conditions of employment, irregular hours, extravagance of means and health, their future prospects, the subject of vocation, Christian-like preparation for marriage, the evils of mixed-marriage, and many other similar topics supply material for an almost endless list of sermons which every young woman will follow with interest, and which cannot fail to influence her present and after life. A meeting without something in the way of instruction attracts a few; one meeting monthly well attended gives

PARISH SOCIETIES

results much more valuable than two or three half-attended.

There is a considerable number of young women willing, anxious, to give some time to real works of zeal. There are several others seeking pastime in less desirable pursuits who can be induced to take part in the activities promoted by the church. A thriving Sodality can become a medium of furthering such undertakings, all of which will serve to give it strength and maintain the interest of its members. It is still better when a variety of employments can be found such as will appeal to the tastes of different members. Some will evince a rare capacity for decorating the altar and looking after the sanctuary furnishings; others are invaluable in the work of instruction whether among illiterate adults or conducting a Sunday school class; others may do much to develop the parish library. Then there are such works of charity as visiting poor patients in public hospitals and in certain homes. Every city pastor is thinking of permanent invalids, never able to leave their homes or perhaps their beds. Often they are poor and unknown. They try to wear in the long hours day after day with little or no means of distraction and rarely a caller. What an event in their sad, dull lives would be the visit of a couple of bright young girls willing to show them a kindness and do something to cheer their loneliness. Needless to add, what a benefit to the young women themselves, particularly to the young women whose homes afford the luxury of ample means and every variety of pleasure. Many of our wealthy or well-to-do Catholics give generously to the poor; how few visit them regularly in their homes, how

SOME PASTOR'S PROBLEMS

fewer still try to understand the lives of the struggling laboring class by putting themselves in contact with the conditions under which their families have to exist. Perhaps they do not dare; the sufferings of the poor might be a reproach to their own self-seeking; they could no longer enjoy their many comforts with the same complacency; on the whole, therefore, it is better not to see or know too much of these people. Now it is precisely for such reasons that young ladies of means and leisure in a Sodality should be induced to visit regularly the needy and suffering. I will go still further. At the present day many young women drive automobiles, and frequently it happens that they are really looking for some place to go. How seldom it occurs to them to share a drive in the open air with some poor creature who has passed months and years with no possible means of getting away from the monotony of her cheerless quarters. Thus, in a large city parish especially, occupations without number can be found to interest members and make them realize that their religion calls for something generous and self-sacrificing on their part.

Aside from the celebration of the greater feasts in honor of Our Lady, it may be well not to insist on assembling the Sodality for extraordinary devotions. Something, however, can easily be done in the way of visits to the Blessed Sacrament in private. There is positively no member who will not undertake as much as this at least once a month; many will do more. A schedule assigning each a different hour, to suit her convenience, will in large parishes secure attendance upon our Lord on the altar during the greater part of the time. The

PARISH SOCIETIES

maintaining of this devotion in vigor requires a very little effort on the part of the Reverend Director.

THE WOMEN

In conducting societies for the benefit of the three classes already dealt with, the great effort lies in finding means of inducing them to attend. In arranging for meetings of the women of the parish it is much less a question of offering inducements than of fixing an hour when all may find it convenient to be present. As a class they need little urging, provided they are free to leave their homes. Whether it be the Confraternity of Christian Mothers, the Apostleship of Prayer, the League of the Sacred Heart, or some other similar organization, matters little, if we can make it possible for all to be present at the monthly Communion and at the regular meeting. Here then is the first question that a director will have to study. The holy-days of obligation, Good Friday, and some other days of devotion which are supposed to claim relief from the stress of home duties will probably afford the best opportunities of assembling for a meeting.

The works of zeal in which members of the organization are asked to take part should consist of the promotion of piety and religious exercises in the home. Discourses prepared with this end in view should aim not merely at *pointing out* what practices members can have cultivated in their homes, but also in *teaching them* in detail how these are to be conducted. Perhaps we all fail to a certain extent in this particular. We exhort; we urge

SOME PASTOR'S PROBLEMS

the necessity and importance of home training in a general way; we deplore the lack of it; we condemn mercilessly the negligence of parents, quite forgetting that reforms rarely come through the most eloquent denunciations of evil, and that a very great deal could be accomplished by any mother who realizes in detail just what is expected of her and knows how to set about it. To explain what I mean I would suggest something like the following as a list of subjects for instruction:

    The morning prayer of young children;
    Morning prayer among the older members;
    Family evening prayer;
    Recitation of the Rosary;
    Prayers before and after meals;
    Prayers upon retiring and rising;
    Prayers in time of temptation and danger, etc.;
    Preparation of children for confession;
    Preparation for first Communion;
    A series of instructions explaining the method of teaching the Catechism in the home;
    How parents may have their children approach the Sacraments regularly;
    Insisting that children make a proper thanksgiving after Communion;
    With what prayer books a family should be provided;
    Singing of hymns in the home;
    Subscribing to and reading Catholic papers;
    Lists of religious books, Catholic stories, etc. to be provided for the home from time to time;
    Supplying the home with sacred pictures, statues, and objects of piety generally;
    Importance of wearing the scapular;

PARISH SOCIETIES

Necessity of correction and punishment;
The duties parents have of training their children in habits of industry;
The danger of acquiring habits of self-indulgence and pleasure-seeking;
Insisting on the observance of proper hours;
Guarding them against dangerous associates and associations;
Children spoiled by too much money;
How parents may encourage home amusements;
What amusements to forbid.

Each of the above is quite sufficient for a distinct instruction, some for two or more. The list, it will be seen at a glance, is far from exhaustive; but it at least suggests the immense possibilities for good lying before us if we can succeed in regularly assembling the mothers of the congregation and make an ordinary reasonable effort to explain to them how to approach the peculiar duties of their position.

Keeping up a general Communion monthly, they will look after themselves with the minimum assistance from the priest in charge. There will always be a few delinquents, however, a few offering pretexts for declining to be enrolled in the society. I know no remedy for this unless it be unremitting attention. The director may find it necessary to call on such members regularly. For the sake of the example they owe their children, no trouble is too great in order to secure their faithful attendance. No matter how well church and school are conducted, there is little prospect of a growing-up family realizing their religious duties if the mother can allow herself to remain indifferent.

SOME PASTOR'S PROBLEMS

Although the number of societies be kept down to four, it is still evident that no one priest can look after all in such a way as to bestow on each the time and energy necessary to their proper maintenance. Wherever possible, it is desirable that the director's attendance be confined to one single organization.

In the confessional we have at our disposal another very effective means of promoting the interests of societies whose purpose is devotional. We shall meet penitents to whom membership in such organizations would be a very decided benefit; we shall meet others already members to whom we can suggest no more practical means of assistance in their peculiar circumstances than strict fidelity to the rules of their society. When all confessors attached to the church understand they are expected to give attention to this line of procedure, much will be done among all classes of the congregation to invigorate the life of and show respect for the different societies and sodalities.

CHAPTER V

CAN MIXED MARRIAGES BE ENTIRELY DONE AWAY WITH?

I

THE Right Reverend Bishop, it was generally understood, exercised a strict policy in the matter of dispensations for mixed marriages, but all the early years of my ministry having been passed in a country parish, where there was no disposition among the faithful to associate with non-Catholics, it was a matter for discussion on theological principles rather than one of any practical interest. Later, on my appointment to a city parish, it became evident that what had afforded hitherto a favorite topic for an after-dinner argument was now to be a real live issue. Even then, although prepared to coöperate scrupulously with the instructions of the bishop, whose policy on this question I had always supported in theory, I nevertheless felt convinced that inevitably every year I should find myself performing a number of marriage ceremonies in the rectory. My parish embraced a considerable portion of the residential section of the city and a number of the families were supposed to be in society, a circumstance which gave confirmation to my forecast of the situation. It never had really occurred to me that there could be such a thing as entirely doing away with the

SOME PASTOR'S PROBLEMS

evil in any locality. I was altogether taken by surprise on facing the issue, on the first occasion presented, to find the bishop quite sanguine of accomplishing something very near to this desirable result. I soon realized that such dispensations were to be of the very rarest occurrence, and that I was expected to play a strenuous part in dealing with the cases that would come under my consideration.

With the bishop only one remedy practically was contemplated. He considered that a Catholic was under the greatest obligation to work for the conversion of the non-Catholic who was proposed as his or her partner for life, that most Catholics did not realize this obligation, or, if they did, had only vague hopes of its fulfilment, and that it devolved upon pastors to bring home to all a sense of this obligation, and to be ready to give to the undertaking every assistance that lay within their power. The laity must be taught faith in the power of prayer to enlighten those who know not God; the individual young person must be taught patience and firmness, and must be ready to make sacrifices when necessary; and the non-Catholic party must be fully instructed in Catholic truth and practices.

Other devices for stemming the evil, now in general practice in large cities, were receiving very little attention in ours. Little or nothing was done to bring young people together by means of pastimes and amusements. Parish dances and parish dancing-halls were forbidden; garden parties, excursions, bazaars, received so little encouragement that they had almost ceased to be heard of; all this in a city where not more than one-eighth of the population was Catholic, and where, through

MIXED MARRIAGES

conditions of employment, our Catholic young people were necessarily making many acquaintances among non-Catholics.

The bishop realized all this but claimed that the one great effectual means of preventing mixed marriages was in the hands of ecclesiastical authority in making them impossible, or, at least, very difficult of attainment. Through this opposition, and with the zealous coöperation of his priests, he hoped to make the faithful understand that the conversion of the non-Catholic party, and not permission to marry him or her in error and prejudice, must be the unwavering aim of every dutiful child of the Church.

One very wholesome result of this stand soon became evident in the view which Catholic families did actually take of the situation. Parents, not too fervent themselves, began to realize that an application for a dispensation would mean endless delay and worry, and very likely disappointment. After all, mixed marriages must be a greater evil than they had ever really understood before. It was time to discourage so much association of their children with those outside the Church. They were more anxious to assemble Catholic young people in their homes and, should there be a member of the family whose marriage with a non-Catholic was actually in contemplation, all, both old and young, saw the advisability of some effort being made to effect his conversion. Then, as a consequence of this change of sentiment, every parish rectory had its list of catchumens under instruction. But it would be tedious to trace in detail the results of the stern policy adopted by the bishop on this very critical question; suffice it to state that within the

SOME PASTOR'S PROBLEMS

space of seven or eight years the toleration of mixed marriages had almost come to an end throughout the diocese, while the number of converts on the occasion of marriage had grown in like proportion.

As far as I am informed, these results were universal. I can speak with accuracy however, only of my own parish. Within its limits during the past nine years the number of marriages in which one of the contracting parties became a convert was one hundred and twenty-two. In that same time three dispensations were granted. In two of these cases it was impossible for the non-Catholic parties to find an opportunity for instruction; the third asked to have his admission to the Church deferred in consideration for his parents. During those nine years two, having been refused dispensations at home, established a domicile in another diocese, and four, on refusal, presented themselves before a Protestant minister. It is worthy of remark that in each of these four cases the non-Catholic party was willing to become a Catholic if requested, and was actually prevented from so doing by the Catholic party—a circumstance much more common than we should have at first imagined. During three years the record was as follows:

1911.
Total number of marriages 23
Marriages with one party a convert 14
Mixed marriages 1

1912.
Total number of marriages 34
Marriages with one party a convert 23
Mixed marriages 0

MIXED MARRIAGES

1913.
Total number of marriages 30
Marriages with one party a convert 15
Mixed marriages 0

These converts include representatives of all classes of society, laboring men, domestic servants, lawyers, physicians, prominent business men, sons and daughters of millionaires. The Methodist, Presbyterian, Baptist, Anglican, and Lutheran denominations, all contributed their share; there were among them Sunday school teachers, Orange Men, Free Masons, sons of Protestant clergymen; one was a son of the Grand Master of the Masons. Not uncommonly embracing the Faith entailed, at least for the time being, the severance of all family ties, the loss of a situation, and even the forfeiting of an inheritance.

The question which naturally arises at this stage is, "What kind of Catholics did they turn out to be?" After the closest observation I have no hesitation in answering that no other class of my congregation afforded so large a proportion of faithful, regular, and exemplary Catholics as those who came into the Church on the occasion of marriage. No one who watched the steadily increasing interest aroused in those new attendants at Mass and devotions, their perseverance assured beyond all hazard, could fail to note that the great force behind this remarkable result was the fervor and example of the Catholic wife or husband who had been instrumental in their conversion. Indeed no inconsiderable gain in events of this kind is the revival of Faith and religious practice in the Catholic party, himself or herself, who realizes the responsibility assumed in bringing another within the Fold. As a general rule, therefore, the perseverance of the convert will depend upon the person whom he marries. Of the one hundred and twenty-two mentioned above only four have become indifferent, and the delinquency of the four is clearly due to the neglect and indifference of their Catholic wives. I have never known a convert to cease the practice of his religious duties who had the good fortune, or rather I should say, the Grace, to share his fate for life with a strict, staunch, devoted Catholic. However unpromising his dispositions may have appeared at the outset, however full of prejudices his training, however uncongenial to his tastes were Catholic sentiments and associations and the routine of the Church's ceremonial, the unwavering example of a true Catholic wife, her unflinching attention to every religious practice, at church or in the home, the surrounding of his life with a real healthy Catholic atmosphere, sooner or later awakened in his heart an appreciation of the Church's teachings, a love for her devotional exercises, and a willingness to conform, even in the minutest detail, to all the observances suggested by her ritual and her unceasing exhortations. Not only that: every pastor has met with the fervent convert whose Catholic husband or wife is anything but exemplary in his or her religious duties. There is no picture more touching than the embarrassment of the neophyte who, for the first time in life, has begun to understand God's ways, and to whom the Sacraments and the Holy Sacrifice of the Mass are already such precious treasures, deploring the indifference, the callousness of her supposed Catholic

MIXED MARRIAGES

husband. There was one young woman whose marriage was followed by the early death of her husband; left without any means, she has remained true to her religion, notwithstanding the bitter opposition of her parents and relatives.

The Ecclesiastical Review has on more than one occasion recorded similar experiences in contributions from the able pen of the Rev. A. B. C. Dunne, of Eau Claire, Wisconsin. No doubt, from many parishes throughout the country the same story can be told. Already I have heard of more than one pastor to whom Father Dunne's articles came as an inspiration, and who, on making the experiment for themselves, announce results equally gratifying. If such experiences point to any general conclusion, it is the possibility of introducing many to the light and practice of the one True Faith through the very circumstances which it was thought could eventuate in nothing but the ever-dreaded mixed marriage. They even seem to suggest that marriage is, in the designs of Providence, one of the principal means of having the Truth accepted among many of those who for generations have been hostile to the Church, and by a still larger number who, through error or indifference to all religious sentiment, would have passed their lives in utter forgetfulness of God and their own eternal interests. In this connexion we are reminded of a remark made by Paulist Fathers who have been engaged for years on non-Catholic Missions, to the effect that ninety-five per cent of their converts are either those intending to marry a Catholic, or who have already been married to a Catholic. Father Dunne, I think, has made a far-reaching observation in his contention, that conversions will be mostly of individuals, and not of masses.

II

The course of instruction preparatory to marriage brings conviction to many, who without more ado ask to be received into the Church. But there is a number, considerably large, for whom this in itself is not sufficient. With the instruction it is necessary that *the non-Catholic understand that marriage is absolutely out of the question if he cannot conscientiously accept Catholic doctrine.* There are many devout Catholics to-day who owe their submission to the Church, after God's grace, to the presence of this condition. Because of its theological, as well as practical aspect, therefore, I shall ask the reader to bear patiently with me in a rather lengthy discussion of its bearings.

We all know Catholics, individuals and families, with whom a mixed marriage would not be contemplated under any consideration. Now, sometimes in these very homes the persistent suitor happens to be a non-Catholic. There is never any doubt in our minds what the outcome will be; sooner or later his conversion is assured, and that before the marriage takes place. A very typical example of this is the incident pictured by Father Sheehan in *My New Curate*. No more unlikely prospect for conversion could have been imagined than that of the gentleman who sought the hand of Britta Campion. Nevertheless no one following that story page by page had any fear for the results. The reader's assurance was based entirely

MIXED MARRIAGES

on his conviction that Britta was too true a Catholic ever to marry one without the Faith. Possessed of a keen, penetrating intelligence, honestly willing to be convinced, receiving every assistance from a learned, zealous pastor, he appeared in the end as far away from the Truth as at the commencement. The patience, the determined attitude of Britta, and the resourcefulness that comes of devotion to a purpose, at length enabled grace to find its way through the mazes of error that clouded this brilliant, but misguided soul. When we shall have succeeded in bringing our Catholic laity to take the same determined stand, conversions will follow just as surely, and the mixed marriage will be a thing of the past. Let us not forget, however, that our success will be limited without this manner of coöperation at the hands of the interested Catholic.

But in this we shall have our difficulties—very great ones—in inspiring our young people with the necessary courage; for we must in all reasonableness take account of the fact that for many young people this event means everything in life. They are not willing to accept the alternative of abandoning the prospect of a marriage which seems in every other way desirable, and which all their friends are recommending. "Suppose," they argue with themselves, "the non-Catholic could not or would not accept the Church's teaching—what has the future to offer me?" Should we not frequently be asking too great a sacrifice? Or can we always assure young people, so situated, that their firmness and patience and prayers will inevitably be rewarded with the conversion of the non-Catholic? An old pastor of my acquaintance was accustomed to give a vigorous as well as a very practical answer to this question. "Why can he not give up his own church and join yours? No Protestant believes that his own denomination alone has the true doctrine; no Protestant is so attached to what he calls his creed; and if he does not care more for you than he does for his own religion, you are better without him." But can we pastors give this guarantee from our own experience? Now let us be accurate. Did any of us ever in all our lives know one man who, having to face the alternative, broke off an engagement with the woman of his choice because his Faith in the *doctrines* of his own denomination were too deep-rooted to be abandoned? Other obstacles which arise, such as the opposition of parents, the hazarding of a business position, the loss of social prestige, though they cannot always be overcome without difficulty, or even heroism, can always be ignored without scruple.

But, suppose we are sure beyond a shadow of doubt that every non-Catholic will eventually enter the Church if the Catholic party make this a condition *sine qua non of* the engagement, there next arises the question, Are we always easy regarding the *sincerity* of his conversion? May we not fear for his motives?

I am quite prepared at this stage to hear advanced the one ever-recurring objection to this manner of dealing. It is expressed popularly in the phrase, "He became a Catholic just to get her"; or the young lady herself will declare, "I would not have him enter the Church just for my sake"; or a third will proffer the statement, "I knew others to become Catholics at the time of marriage and give it

MIXED MARRIAGES

up afterward." Now, it might be well to remind our good Catholic people occasionally that no one is admitted to the Church unless a priest has first pronounced upon his dispositions, and assumed responsibility for the very serious step to be taken. Every conversion is a conversion to a life of grace. Admission to the Church is admission to the Sacraments, and any trifling in such matters on the part of God's ministers would be a line of conduct too shocking to contemplate.

It is quite true that we have known persons to enter the Church and at some later date cease to practice their religious duties. But if our experience has been at all extended, we have also known some to embrace Catholicity with no other incentive than the purest love of the Truth, who are no longer known to the Fold. My own personal experience is that the latter class supplies a larger portion of perversions than the former. Moreover, we have seen Catholics from infancy, well instructed, known for their fervor at the time of First Communion and Confirmation, and even in early manhood, who long since have ceased to be known as faithful children of the Church. Of all three classes it may be said that grace was abused, or a protecting hand was wanting in the time of danger, or the foundations of Faith were not laid sufficiently deep to withstand the mighty blasts of after years.

Our objector continues, "He certainly would never have become a Catholic if he had not wished to marry a Catholic girl." Very true; nor is it at all likely that we ourselves should possess the inestimable gift of Faith if our parents had not possessed it before us. But by the merciful dispensation of God they have led us to a knowledge of His Truth—to see the one True Light; now we would die for it at any time. And are our motives for believing to be distrusted because, when we were young and incapable of discerning, we learned our Catechism at the request of those whom we loved? Is a man's conviction, then, to be impugned because he began the examination of Catholic doctrine at the urging of one for whom he had the highest regard? He does not embrace the Faith *because his fiancee obliges him to do so. At her request he agrees to examine the claims of the Church.* He lays aside his prejudices; he is open to conviction, and, through the grace of God, the clear presentation of eternal truth enlightens his soul. His desire to make that girl his wife it was that turned him to study Catholic teaching. There was his opportunity; it was God's way of calling him; and we might add without severity, woe to the young woman who would stand in the way of his responding to it.

Theologically the question resolves into this: Is there more hope for the real conversion of a person who has some worldly motive to induce him to enter the Church than for one who is not actuated by any such motive? Is he more likely to discover what is in reality the true light who from lower motives is extremely desirous of doing so, than he who has no wish to escape from what is in reality darkness and error? Granted an equal intelligence and the same course of instruction to two non-Catholics, both genuinely honest in their intention, one however having everything to gain by becoming a Catholic, the other absolutely nothing, can I believe that the former enjoys more favorable dis-

MIXED MARRIAGES

positions for enlightenment from on high than the latter?

In ignorance of any authoritative decision on the subject, and with the fullest submission to any pronouncement that may be forthcoming, I venture to answer, "Yes," and for the following reasons.

1. Our Divine Lord throughout the Gospel commends a readiness to believe. To appreciate the significance of these words of our Lord the reader has only to recall Cardinal Newman's wonderful sermon entitled, "Dispositions for Faith."

2. A man's efforts to discover the truth will be in keeping with his desire to possess it. As Cardinal Newman says, when a man is really anxious to know God's teaching, he will be "on the lookout" for information, arguments, proofs; and his very exertions, with this end in view, will lead him face to face with the truth.

3. An ardent desire to be admitted to the Church, no matter from what motive it springs, will of itself be most effectual in dissipating the mists of prejudice.

4. Faith is the work not only of the *intellect* but also of the *will*. "Revelanti Deo intellectus et voluntatis obsequium praestare tenemur." [1] "Si quis dixerit assensum fidei Christianae non esse liberum, sed argumentis humanae rationis necessario produci, anathema sit." [2]

5. In ninety-nine cases out of a hundred the modern non-Catholic's objections to the Catholic Church were not arrived at by a process of reasoning, nor will they be removed by a logical argumentation alone.

[1] Vat. Con.
[2] Ibid.

SOME PASTOR'S PROBLEMS

6. God's ordinary means of propagating Christian truth and practice is through the Christian family, where certainly the study of religous doctrine is supported by our affection and esteem for our parents, and by the desire to believe and practise what they have believed and practised.

So much for the theological aspects of the case taken in general. Now, if the example be of a man who has asked to be instructed because the young lady positively refused to marry anyone not a Catholic, is not his willingness to be guided blindly by a devout member of the Church, in itself an act of submission to the Church's authority? Is not his decision to offer no opposition to the teaching of the Church, to do everything in his power to accept her teaching, and to obey her laws, a state of mind upon which heaven will look with favor? At the same time, when the young lady is ready to make such sacrifices for the cause of God, is she not likely to be rewarded by the man of her choice receiving the light to understand and accept God's will?

Up to this point we have been discussing the case where a *real conversion* is to be effected, where a person has fixed religious convictions, and where our task is to convince him that these must be abandoned because there is only one religion which comes from God. Such a person in our day is comparatively rare. But, if a prospective marriage can be a potent factor in the conversion of one who has distinct religious convictions, and who cannot appreciate the claims of the Catholic Church, it is easy to understand its legitimate power

MIXED MARRIAGES

when the non-Catholic is deterred, not by any positive beliefs which claim his adherence, but by one or more of a variety of causes which are associated only indirectly, if at all, with the study of religion. We really make a mistake in speaking of these latter as converts at all. Many know as little of the doctrines of their own sect as they do of Catholic doctrine. They have no more difficulty in accepting the Church's teachings than has the neglected Catholic who is prevailed upon to prepare for First Communion and Confirmation at the age of twenty. The only difficulty is in having them give their attention to it, and nothing secures this attention so effectually as its being a *sine qua non* of their prospective marriage. Others do not wish to hear "conversion" proposed because of the time and trouble, perhaps delay, the instruction will entail. A dispensation would be so much more convenient for all concerned. Others, not only have never given any thought to the subject of religion, but have never even allowed the practice of religious duties to interfere with the comfort of their lives. Then there are those who do not wish to think of Catholicity because of unreasoned prejudices, or an unenlightened bigotry, or a loyalty to the Church of their parents and ancestors. Now any one of those may one day become a sincere, fervent Catholic; but it is quite clear that progress in that direction will be lamentably slow if there be no stimulus but the cold, naked, logical exposition of her teachings. It is the *will* that must be moved. There is not one of those apparently insuperable obstacles which will not tumble down and disappear before the longing for the hand of one who can be won only on condition that such obstacles be removed forever. It is not a conversion at all, it is simply teaching Catechism; leading them for the first time in life to think seriously of God and another world; to understand something of sin and its punishment; having them commence to pray morning and evening and pay some attention to the observance of Sunday. There is no pardoning the Catholic young woman who, having it in her power to accomplish all this, neglects to do so, preferring rather to share her fate for life with a man who has as little regard for his eternal salvation as the pagan of darkest Africa.

It has been the aim of previous paragraphs to show that the wish to marry a Catholic may, with the grace of God, be the most common and most effectual means of bringing those outside the Church to understand and accept her doctrine. *It is not, however, the greatest work which such marriages accomplish in attaching converts to the Faith.* It is an easier task, from the point of view of human effort, to secure the submission of the non-Catholic, to instruct him, and admit him to the Church, than to keep him faithful to the practice of his religion until death. All the religious instruction which we ourselves received in youth has had much less to do with the faithfulness and fervor of our lives than have the solicitude and guardianship of our parents for years afterward. Similarly with the adult convert: no thoroughness of instruction previous to his reception contributes so much to his faithfulness through life as the example and influence of the devout Catholic wife or husband. For want of such protection many a convert who entered the Church

MIXED MARRIAGES

after a long and thoughtful examination of her claims—perhaps also at the cost of great sacrifices—later in life gradually fell away and sank into a hopeless indifference. We preach, in season and out of season, that the Faith cannot be preserved without the influence of the Christian family and home. We insist that no efficiency in our Catholic schools can ever take the place of the training in the home. What is so indispensably necessary to develop a religious spirit in the heart of a child cannot fail to be an all-important agency in developing the Faith of the adult neophyte. Or, again, in our anxiety for some Catholic young man who is acquiring habits of recklessness, or is no longer amenable to good influence, we unanimously declare that everything will depend on the person whom he marries. We thereby bear testimony to the important part which marriage will play in having him attend to his religious duties. Strange to say, no one ever seems to doubt the sincerity of his religious practices under such influences. If therefore marriage has been the sole redemption of one who enjoyed every early advantage, is its protection not still more necessary for a convert? One of our pastors goes so far as to say, "I do not care to have anything to do with a convert if he is not already, or about to be, married to a Catholic."

III

When it is generally understood that dispensations will be rarely granted, is there not a danger that a Catholic intending to marry a non-Catholic will agree to the ceremony being performed by a

SOME PASTOR'S PROBLEMS

Protestant minister or civil magistrate? On first sight we should be inclined to say, "Yes, most certainly."

In every discussion on the advisability of strict regulations against mixed marriages this objection occurs to all. Fears of such consequences have counseled more than one bishop to proceed with caution, much as he would wish to attack the evil by offering every opposition in his power. Text-books on theology seem to hint that in the face of such a possibility a generous mitigation of the law is justifiable. In this, however, as in everything else, the discretion to be exercised in dealing with a given individual case may be something altogether different from the attitude of mind required in deciding what line of conduct to adopt when dealing with a permanent condition of things. The strictest administrator will at times realize the advisability of making an exception. The question here is not what is wisest under certain circumstances in a particular case, but how will the population of a diocese be affected by realizing that mixed marriages as a rule are not tolerated, and that dispensations for such will rarely, if ever, be granted.

No one doubts that a readiness to grant dispensations and the consequent increase in the number of mixed marriages in a community tend to lessen the horror and odium in which such unions are accustomed to be held. According as a people lose that horror for mixed marriages in general will they also lose their horror for mixed marriages performed outside the Church. Or to take a paralleled condition: we know that in some countries or provinces Catholics have never been known to

MIXED MARRIAGES

eat meat on Friday under any circumstances; while in others they have been accustomed to obtain dispensations for various reasons according to the judgment of the pastor. Have we any doubt at all among which of those peoples we are more likely to meet with unwarranted violations of the law of abstinence, or at least a decided laxity in its observance?

This, however, is reasoning *a priori*. The question can be answered satisfactorily only by collecting statistics, by finding out in accurate figures from different dioceses or cities what have been the respective results of strict and lenient tendencies in the granting of dispensations for mixed marriages. Complete information in details of this nature is something which Catholic parishes and dioceses rarely possess. That we take our beliefs on the authority of an Infallible Guide may account for our dispositions and practices in these matters, but certainly inaccuracy of statistics is a very common feature in the methods of Church administration in use among us. Is it a fact that in those dioceses where dispensations have been granted readily, marriages outside the Church have been done away with, or even considerably reduced in number? Personally I have never known one such result, nor have I ever spoken to anyone who did. In dioceses where dispensations have been rarely granted has the number of marriages outside the Church increased? This discussion became so lively in our diocese that some of us made a practice of consulting the civil registers at the end of each year. What was our astonishment to find, time after time, that during the years in which the bishop had practically

SOME PASTOR'S PROBLEMS

closed the door on dispensations the number of marriages outside the Church *showed a very marked decrease.*

IV

In conclusion, allow me to add that in suggesting greater efforts to convert the non-Catholic on the occasion of marriage I am well aware that I am imposing endless tasks on the already over-burdened lives of our pastors and assistants. No doubt the failure to accomplish all that could have been desired is due chiefly to want of time and convenience to give the necessary instruction. Would it not be advisable in every city to commit all the work of instruction to one priest, who would be free to give all his attention to this task? This plan, besides insuring opportunities to deal with all, and besides the efficiency which leisure for one line of work will guarantee, would also secure the very great advantage of economy of time and energy. One teacher would then be occupied regularly with a large class instead of a number of teachers being each employed with one or two pupils.

CHAPTER VI

INSTRUCTING CONVERTS

THE term "convert," in the great majority of cases to which it is usually applied, is a misnomer. To give a non-Catholic a copy of the "Faith of Our Fathers" or "Catholic Belief," expecting results therefrom is, unless in very exceptional cases, not merely futile but a mistake. To suppose the ordinary man or woman of the world will seek admission to the Church and live the life of a faithful Catholic after listening to sermons for non-Catholics seven successive days is—barring the interposition of miracles of grace—to expect the impossible. Few of us hope ever to see an example of it.

In the strict and ordinary acceptation of the term a convert is one who, having fixed religious convictions and pursuing them in the earnest desire to save his soul, is brought to an examination of Catholic teaching, discovers the errors of his former position, and embraces the one true faith. This, however, describes not one in ten of the large numbers who break off connection with Protestant denominations to become Catholics. These are not converts in the strict sense because they have had no convictions to give up, or even modify. Our task in being called upon to instruct them is not that of correcting erroneous beliefs, adding proofs to show them the fallacy of their convictions, but simply informing them what are the truths every Christian

SOME PASTOR'S PROBLEMS

must believe and practice. Theirs is not the result of years of heterodox instruction, of accepting misrepresentations of Christian teaching, but of little or no Christian instruction whatever; not of being misinformed, but of not being informed at all; not of error, but of ignorance. In dealing, therefore, with nine out of every ten the instruction is practically the same as would be given to a class of children preparing for first Communion or confirmation.

Or, let us take another case to all intents and purposes parallel. Through the neglect of parents, Catholic in name and profession, a boy grows up without religious instruction or practice. At the age of eighteen or twenty, influenced by the example of associates, or urged by some distant Catholic relative, or perhaps beginning to pay attention to some Catholic young lady, he calls on the pastor and asks to be prepared for confession and Communion. We all know exactly what to do; who would dream of having him commence by reading the "Faith of Our Fathers" or some other work of controversy? Yet in his attitude towards fundamental Christian teaching such a young man differs little or nothing from three-fourths of all who call themselves Protestants, except in his being free from blind prejudice against the claims of Catholicity. They are no more capable of sustaining an argument in opposition to any particular article of the creed than he. The proportion of non-Catholics answering this description is on the increase in a country where only twenty-two out of a total of seventy-four millions profess to be members of any religious denomination, and in which nearly four million children receive no religious instruction whatever.

Those of us whose position imposes the task of

INSTRUCTING CONVERTS

instructing several adult catechumens year after year are, I venture to say, quite agreed upon this view of the case. During our early experiences we were wont to prepare ourselves for the strenuous undertaking of presenting arguments in defense of the Real Presence, devotion to Our Lady, Purgatory, Indulgences, with a force that our "convert" would have difficulty in gainsaying, and we looked upon his ready and reticent acquiescence as a clever deceitfulness to keep us in the dark or a modest means of flattering our vanity. Great as was the confidence reposed in the strength of our position, it was too soon to expect a complete dislodgment of his intelligent, long-formed convictions. It was only with repeated experiences that we began to realize that his acceptance of our explanations was perfectly genuine because there were actually no convictions to dislodge. It was the very first time he had ever given the question any serious thought at all, and in accepting found just as little difficulty as does the Catholic child who for the first time hears of purgatory from his parents or teacher.

The priest unprepared for such surprises will not wait long to find that his class of non-Catholic adults have never grasped with anything like accuracy the doctrine of the Incarnation, in which all Christians profess to believe. Soon afterwards, he will be heard remarking that, though every one he is instructing claims to have been baptized, rarely does he meet one with any conception of the purpose of Baptism. The ignorance of Catholic teaching which Protestants of one denomination or another evince, is really not so striking as the ordinary Protestant's ignorance of the tenets of his own particular denomination.

SOME PASTOR'S PROBLEMS

Somehow or other, we are disposed to concede to our separated brethren a superiority in one respect, —a decided familiarity with the Bible. We assume that it must be so; on their own profession it is the adequate explanation as well as the basis of all religious belief and practice: the Bible is their Sunday-school text-book and devotional manual when attending services; it is the only book to be used on occasions of family prayer. Then we have met from time to time a zealous church member who quoted scriptural texts with wonderful facility. But it is only when interrogating the rank and file— as a catechumen class gives opportunity of doing— that we realize that the rank and file know nothing of the Bible. Whether or not the Protestant laity of older countries for two or three centuries after the Reformation were trained to a familiarity with its contents, beyond all question the Methodist, Presbyterian and Baptist Sunday schools of our day are accomplishing nothing in the way of giving their pupils an acquaintance with the writings they speak of as the Sacred Text.

With an adult or class of adults, knowing so little of even the fundamental truths, the work of instruction is nothing more or less than an ordinary catechism class and the text-book just such as best suits parochial school children. Objections ordinarily raised by non-Catholics under instruction no priest finds difficulty in answering. They are usually the same half-dozen, more or less, and have been raised and answered a thousand times before. The party demanding the explanation has never examined the matter very closely himself, but happens to know that his parents or non-Catholic friends were given to emphasize the absurdity, or perhaps

INSTRUCTING CONVERTS

the iniquity, of such teaching and practice. If he be a victim of deep-seated prejudices, the most lucid and convincing refutation will probably prove ineffective. I am speaking, of course, of usual experiences; now and then we have to deal with a student intelligent, studious, advancing arguments that require a comprehensive grasp, supported by wide reading of works of history. For such we have to prepare.

Success in the instruction of adults depends very much less on deep theological learning and capacity for controversy than upon a self-denying faithfulness to the task undertaken. Regularity and punctuality are strictly essential. If Wednesday evening, eight o'clock, be the hour arranged, make every effort to be free at that hour. Absence because of an urgent sick-call, or some pressing engagement unforeseen, our catechumen will readily excuse. When possible, notify him beforehand of the disappointment; when not possible, soon after, and then proceed to arrange another hour at the earliest convenience to all concerned. Never allow him to suppose for a moment that you are not keenly interested in his case; let him feel he is always welcome, that you are anxiously awaiting his call. Should his absence once or twice give reason to suspect indifference, or negligence, or some unwholesome influence, take the trouble of enquiring either by telephone, or by a note, or by a personal call. Causes there may be, both natural and supernatural, which make this little encouragement a matter of absolute necessity. It is probably attention to this detail, or lack of it, which accounts for the extraordinary phenomenon, so often observable, that while one pastor has always a class of converts to instruct

SOME PASTOR'S PROBLEMS

and is constantly admitting new members to the Church, his neighbor or successor similarly circumstanced, is without any. God only knows how many there are among us living and dying out of the faith through our neglect of making the effort which this practice involves.

In a city parish especially, the number may become so large as to suggest the difficulty of want of time. One evening a week is quite often enough to call the class together. Oftener will not allow sufficient leisure, all things considered, for the preparation they are expected to make in the way of private study, reading, etc. They must have time to digest. Barring the case in which one or the other catechumen is obliged to be at work during the hour of class, there is no necessity for individual instruction. Each will make greater progress by attending a class, if for no other reason, than that the teacher can afford to be more generous of himself on a whole evening set aside for this duty than during the hour he tries to spare for the accommodation of someone in particular. That all have not commenced together will be found to offer no appreciable disadvantage, provided the class proceeds continuously one chapter after another; he or she who arrives for the fifteenth or twentieth or thirtieth chapter will later on receive instruction in the first or second or third. Some there will be who, through timidity or reserve, will insist upon the privilege of private instruction. I take the liberty of advising the young priest to pay no attention to such requests. The timidity, though quite natural, very soon disappears. The most reluctant to join the class are usually the most enthusiastic shortly afterwards. A large class becomes

INSTRUCTING CONVERTS

attractive. The presence of eight or ten others, coming from different denominations, all interested in the Catholic teaching, is a real inspiration, and catechumens at all sincere invariably find a discussion under such circumstances intensely interesting. So much is this the case that several ask to be allowed to continue attending after being admitted to the Sacraments, and when the course of instruction has been pronounced complete.

An explanation of the dogmas of religion, however long and thorough, a painstaking drill in every point of doctrine which the Catechism takes note of, are far from being the only training necessary to the formation of a practical Christian. They alone who are Catholic in heart and will and practice and life as well as in understanding and knowledge, are Catholics worthy of the name. The catechumen, therefore, must be drilled in the practice of Catholic devotions no less than in the understanding of Catholic truth. There is nothing in connection with the instruction of a convert so important to remember as this. From the very commencement individual members of the class should be urged to assist at Mass (prayerbook in hand and seated near the sanctuary to observe the ceremonies as closely as possible), to attend Benediction, Vespers, the Stations of the Cross, and other public devotions so far as convenience will allow; to be faithful to morning and evening prayer, and, when no serious objection is offered, to the form prescribed in an ordinary prayerbook or catechism; to cultivate the practice of prayer before and after meals, etc., to abstain Fridays, and, if the season is at hand, to do something toward the observance of abstinence in Lent. Later on such devotions as the Rosary,

SOME PASTOR'S PROBLEMS

the use of Holy Water, etc., may be explained and their adoption prudently suggested.

The non-Catholic honestly seeking the truth, who gives himself generously to those practices of devotion, and who after a reasonable time still experiences real difficulties in accepting the Church's teachings, is a phenomenon to be met with very rarely indeed. The longer we are engaged in this feature of parochial work, the more we shall be convinced that the number debarred from entering the Church through difficulties in accepting her doctrines is small compared with those who recoil from the observance of her laws. There are those who have been admitted to the Sacraments, persevered for a time, and afterwards fallen away; the event is often referred to as an evidence of lack of conviction from the beginning; nineteen times out of twenty the continued effort and the self-denial required to live the life of an every-day practical Catholic is the explanation, and fifteen times out of twenty not fasting or going to confession was the stumbling-block, but the grave obligation of assisting at Mass fifty-two Sunday mornings every year. We must remember that the religion of Jesus Christ has emblazoned on its standard: "If any man will come after Me, let him deny himself, take up his cross and follow Me," and we are never assured of the fitness of an applicant until his conduct gives reasonable evidence of a willingness to follow that standard. It is, therefore, usually wise to postpone the reception of a convert who has not been seen at Mass regularly for a year or the greater part of it, or who acknowledges a decided reluctance to spending a few minutes on his knees every morning and evening. If the non-Catholic

INSTRUCTING CONVERTS

in question had hitherto been deeply sincere in his religious convictions, if he had been faithful in the observance of everything enjoined by the denomination to which he professed to belong, if Sunday had always been for him a day of church-going and devotion, and if his only objection to being a Catholic arose from difficulties in its doctrine, we might expect that, these difficulties once removed, his earnestness in the welfare of his soul would insure a ready correspondence with any practice which faith in the Church inspires. But this is the exceptional case. To give the ordinary "convert" a series of instructions in catechism, to insist on his knowing certain forms of prayer by rote to prepare him for confession and admit him to the Sacraments without any attention to his devotional practices, is a process which, with God's grace, may sometimes produce good results, but generally speaking, unless he be about to marry one capable of guaranteeing his faithfulness, it should not surprise us to find him shortly afterwards very much as he was before. We, whose inestimable privilege it has been to belong to the fold from infancy, can hardly forget that something more than a Catechism class was in force to make us practical Catholics; we can hardly forget that unceasing watchfulness over our daily prayers and attendance at Mass, those never-failing suggestions and reminders and corrections to which, after God, we owe in great measure whatever faith or fervor or practice it is our blessing to possess.

It is also advisable that the convert's practice of Catholicity be confined almost entirely to the exercises which constitute the routine of a Catholic's life. A round of missions, forty hours, sol-

SOME PASTOR'S PROBLEMS

emn Masses, attractive church music and sermons at that stage may, to a certain extent, carry him away, but only to leave disappointment and dissatisfaction with the more or less prosaic occurrence at which he will be expected to assist regularly later on. The academy girl who is converted and continues as a devout Catholic within the convent walls, and who soon after falls away, is common enough to excite considerable comment. Have we not here the explanation? Amid the imposing grandeur of a chapel, the richness and decoration of its sanctuary, the charm of music and the impressiveness of religious events, it is easy to be sincerely pious and devout; the practice of religion bereft of all these extraordinary stimulants, which will probably be her lot on returning to the world, demands a faith and determination and exertion for which she is not prepared.

All these contentions anticipate to a certain degree the theological tenet that conversion to the faith concerns the will as well as the intellect. In dealing with a catechumen of the most common type, securing the consent of the will would seem to be the one great desideratum. An intellectual assent is rarely possible with him who, through interest or prejudice, is determined not to enter the Church. On the other hand, a desire to become a Catholic from some interested motive, provided that desire implies an honest intention to yield to the Church's claims *on their own merit,* is a disposition which God will bless with light to know His law and willingness to embrace it. If of our efforts God's judgments should reward only those proceeding from the purest motives, with absolutely

INSTRUCTING CONVERTS

no alloy of worldly self-interest, how small would be our our store for eternity! When the will of our pupil, therefore, interposes no obstacles, our task of instructing is easy. A very large percentage of present-day "converts"—some say ninety or ninety-five—are admitted to the Church on the occasion of marriage; it will probably always be so, in other countries no less than in this, and the explanation is as above. Through the Catholic party's refusing to marry one not of the faith, the non-Catholic is disposed to place no obstacle to the acceptance of the truth. The part played by the Catholic party taking this stand, therefore, is the all-important one of securing the coöperation of the will.

Behind all this is the doctrine enunciated by Dr. Orestes A. Brownson as follows: "To believe is normal, to disbelieve is abnormal. When the mind is in its normal state, nothing more is ever needed for belief than the removal of the obstacles interposed to believing; for if we consider it, the mind was created for truth. Truth is its object, and it seeks and accepts it instinctively, as the new-born child seeks the mother's breast, from which it draws its nourishment. Place the mind and truth face to face, with nothing interposed between them, and the truth evidences itself to the mind, and the mind accepts it, without seeking or needing any further reason. The assent termed knowledge follows immediately from the joint forces of the intelligible object and the intelligent subject. So in belief. Practically, it is never a reason for believing, but the removal of reasons against believing, that is demanded. Hence, we always believe what a man tells us, when we have no reason for not believing him; and the business of life could not go on were it otherwise. For belief reason never requires anything but the mutual presence, with nothing interposed between them, of the credible object and the crediting subject. Truth needs no voucher, and when immediately presented to the mind, affirms itself. The will may be perverse, and withdraw the intellect from the contemplation of truth; prejudice or passion may darken the understanding, so that it does not for the moment see or recognize the object; but, whenever the truth is immediately present, and reason looks it full in the face, it knows that it is truth without further evidence, without anything intrinsic to prove that it is truth."

Will our convert persevere? Who is going to answer when so many sons and daughters of Catholic parents grow careless and renounce the faith? Many, and these intelligent men and women, have embraced the faith from deep-rooted conviction, from motives strictly sincere, perhaps at the cost of great sacrifices, and afterwards denied that same faith. But having given every care to prepare a person for admission to the Church, is there anything more we must do to insure his continuance therein? Very often little or nothing. Often it would seem as if our mission ended there. This, nevertheless, appears certain:—much more depends upon the influences which surround the "convert" after, than upon the thoroughness of his training before, his conversion. If, through marriage or otherwise, he is, in God's Providence, brought under the influence of a wholesome, fervent, exemplary Catholic practice, we have little to fear; if

INSTRUCTING CONVERTS

not, who shall answer for him? One duty assuredly is ours:—should occasion call for it, no effort must be spared to dissuade him from contemplating marriage with one not of the faith.

CHAPTER VII

THE COUNTRY PASTOR'S WEEKDAY

I

IT seems a common assumption that the priest engaged in parish work is often without employment. The country pastors, or assistant especially, is supposed to deserve our sympathy. He also receives generous advice in his struggles against the dreaded ennui necessarily attending a life with so few activities to engage his attention. Is all this in accord with actual fact? And if so, does it not seem somewhat at variance with our preconceived notions of the sacerdotal ministry? A priest's life, we feel, should be one of untiring zeal; and great zeal supposes, above everything else, energy, toil, weariness, with a multiplication of duties so continued as to allow neither time nor strength for their accomplishment.

We are hearing constantly of the appalling scarcity of priests. We are asked to believe that immense harvests of immortal souls are lost eternally because of this scarcity. It is urged that every conceivable sacrifice be made to increase their number; and in the same breath we are told that the most distressing experiences of those actually engaged in the ministry are due to the long hours they spend with nothing to do, week after week, year after year. Is there not some note of incongruity

RURAL PASTOR'S WEEKDAY

in these several references to prevailing conditions? Is it that the shepherd's life is one of patient waiting rather than of absorbing toil? Is it that he who is placed in the watchtower of Israel must understand that the duties of vigilance obliging him never to desert his post require little activity in the exercise thereof?

The professional man and the man of business equally with the laborer are called to continuous duty day after day. A definite plan of occupation holds them there from morning till night. Is it really so with the workday of a priest? Does he rise from breakfast with a vision of eight or ten hours of engagements awaiting him before his day is completed? Of Saturday afternoon and Sunday this is possibly true. What of the remaining five days? Fifteen or twenty minutes over the morning paper, if it arrive early; occasionally some sick parishioner expecting a call; perhaps once a week an hour in the school, if there be one; a letter to write now and then—what else?

The case is not unknown of a young assistant being shown his room and informed of the hours at which meals are served in the rectory. As time goes on he understands that his services will be required on Saturday afternoon and Sunday, on the day when the children make their monthly confession, and occasionally when a distant sick-call is to be attended. For the rest, it becomes evident that the fewer acquaintances he makes among members of the congregation, the more satisfactory his conduct is in the eyes of superiors. Such instances are tremendously sad, whether we consider the interests of the young man himself, the congregation, or, above all, the one who so regulates his hours of employment. Is this the kind of life in preparation for which he had given years of the closest application? Are there really no other duties awaiting him?

All depends upon the size and character of the parish, is the answer we naturally expect to hear. In some parishes, occupations of every kind press upon pastor and assistant at every hour; in others, few or none. Is that a full explanation of the case?

Some priests are among the busiest of men: their days are always full. Is this due to the size and peculiar character of the parish, or to themselves? To have the repute of being faithful in the discharge of every duty which comes to us, and nothing more, is after all a very questionable recommendation. It almost reminds us of the advice an American humorist gives to young men: "Don't wait for things to turn up; turn them up yourself. You might as well sit down on a stone in the middle of a meadow and wait for a cow to back up to be milked." To have scrupulously and promptly attended every sick-call, no matter how trying the circumstances; to be willing to hear every confession that comes, no matter at what hour; to have always prepared the Sunday sermon carefully— these things describe a conscientious workman, but they are not all that are necessary in him who must lead and rule and guide, who feels a responsibility before God for every soul committed to his charge. It is one thing to do every task assigned us; another to see and do everything that should be done.

Generally speaking, the man who is always busy is the man *who can see things to do*. If there are pastors or assistants to whom the great problem

RURAL PASTOR'S WEEKDAY

during a large portion of every week is the problem of getting in their time, who will say how much of this embarrassment is due to their not seeing the work which lies before them undone? The most active pastor of my acquaintance says that for several years in the ministry his flock numbered less than sixty families, and even then he was always busy. It is commonly admitted that the English diocese have at once the smallest Catholic congregations and the hardest-working priests in Europe. Of a certain farmer, whose success is of nation-wide repute, it has been said, "Ordinarily such a farm as his requires three or four men; give him fifteen men, and he will find profitable work for them all." This probably exemplifies what makes for efficiency in any industrial undertaking, and most probably describes a capacity more or less requisite in the administration of a parish. A pastor in a neighboring city, whose census enrolls 2,300 souls, importunes the bishop to keep him constantly provided with a staff of five assistants, and certainly, if each one covers as much ground month by month as does the pastor himself, there are no hours for ennui in or about that rectory. No greater blessing can overtake a young priest than the privilege of associating with a pastor who allows no form of parish duty to be neglected, who is ever discovering new objects of zeal within the limits of his parish, and who has a capacity for dealing with them.

II

Broad fields of inquiry are suggested here. It is evident that all ordained for the Altar are not

SOME PASTOR'S PROBLEMS

equally gifted in this respect. Are there not many who, under proper guidance and tuition, would acquire this capacity in a very high degree, and who, left to their own unaided resources, spend long years in the ministry with little thought of anything beyond the commonest routine? Are there any of the newly ordained so unpromising as not to improve very materially under such tuition? Are there any among the most gifted who might not have done much better?

Then there is the other question—with how much of this training has the average candidate for the ministry been equipped in the past? Has he entered upon the exercise of his calling with anything like a complete description of the various duties awaiting him, and with a thorough understanding of how his days and hours may be filled with priestly occupations? I recall here the frequent remark of an old and worthy pastor in words such as follow: "It has always been a matter of wonder to me that some definite plan of work has not been prescribed for us by ecclesiastical authorities. When Monday morning comes, what is laid out for us? Absolutely nothing. We are free. The active man may plunge into a thousand things; the less active man may attempt none. To be told there are many things we could and should do within that period, and to have those duties imposed upon us at a given day or hour, in accordance with a regular schedule, would inspire a sense of obligation altogether different." Such a regular succession of duties most likely has not been prescribed at any time or place by Church authority, the intention evidently being to leave all this to the personal responsibility of the priest. Autonomy in parochial administration

RURAL PASTOR'S WEEKDAY

would seem to be a cardinal principle. But as a matter of guidance, of direction, of suggestion, we might reasonably expect to hear of such schedules being framed in ecclesiastical seminaries and by writers of pastoral theology. Or, is it contended that this line of instruction is beyond the scope of a seminary's undertaking? Cardinal Newman says that St. Philip Neri in his formation period came successively under the influence of Benedictines, Dominicans, and Jesuits; and he adds: "From the first he learned what to be, from the second what to do, and from the third how to do it." Seminaries of the past seem to have held that their functions were confined to the first, largely to the exclusion of the second and third. If the study of theology and the exercises of sacerdotal formation fill up the limited time at the disposal of the seminary, there is still some further provision needed to guarantee success in the ministry.

III

But let us not get away from the rural pastor, whose many idle hours we have taken for granted. His congregation is made up of country residents, or it is partly country and partly village or town. He is a young man entering upon his first charge, and will not object to having the subject opened for discussion. We may take the liberty at the outset of warning him against the fundamental mistake of attempting a variety of organizations similar to what he has seen in operation in city parishes. Sooner or later he will discover that most of them are unnecessary, if not positively hurtful

SOME PASTOR'S PROBLEMS

in his new surroundings, and that his activities hereafter must be along lines altogether different.

His forenoons will be easily provided for. An average of one, weekly, will be taken up with Mass and confessions in the mission church, a station, or funeral, or a requiem. Two or more will be required to prepare the weekly sermons, and one to visit the school if there is one. Bringing the sacraments to the aged and invalided—a portion of his flock that should have every encouragement to receive the sacraments frequently; reserving an hour occasionally for looking up a *casus conscientiae*, for book-keeping, correspondence, and minor details of a business nature, with the time taken up answering office calls, will leave little or no leisure in the hours before midday.

Allowing one afternoon for rest, recreation, or visiting a neighboring pastor, the problem is reduced to finding employment for the remaining four. While in the course of the year a variety of duties present themselves as different circumstances arise, there are some requiring regular attention almost every week. Chief of these are the catechizing of children, instruction of the adult population, instruction and reception of converts, regular visitation of families and individuals.

IV

It can hardly be controverted that so long as there is one member of the flock without the knowledge of religion which every good Catholic should possess, the pastor's work is not done; nor has he to look elsewhere for pastime. It is commonly assumed that Catholics in country districts, whether

RURAL PASTOR'S WEEKDAY

children or adults, suffer through want of instruction. Instinctively almost, we are disposed to excuse their shortcomings because of their lack of opportunities. Now let us remember what this means. In the very parishes in which a priest's life is nigh unto unbearable through want of occupation, we are to expect a laity in ignorance of the necessary truths of religion! They are supposed to have failed to learn them because there was no Catholic school, as if it were to Sisters of religious communities and to young girls with a teacher's certificate that the Divine commission was given to *go forth and teach*. In European countries considered Catholic, we hear of great majorities of the people grown indifferent, paying no attention to the Church's laws, manifesting no anxiety for the eternal welfare of themselves or their children. The explanation is always the same: a masonic government fifty years ago, or at some past date, abolished Catholic schools. In none of those centres has the Church been closed, or the priest forbidden the exercise of his ministry. Given a compact body of peasantry, whether residing on their respective farms or grouped in villages, as obtains in those countries, and a priest free to move among them seven days in the week, spending terms of ten, twenty, or thirty years in one parish, and it does seem very extraordinary, to say the least, that people so situated are not taught the truths of religion and taught them well.

Although in most places the common practice is to attempt something in the way of a Catechism class on Sunday, it may reasonably be questioned if it were not better, all things considered, to regard the catechizing of children as altogether a

SOME PASTOR'S PROBLEMS

weekday duty. No matter what the conditions, the pastor has little opportunity or leisure to meet all the children on Sunday; and substitutes are of very doubtful assistance. Moreover, assembling children on Sunday afternoon deprives parents of the most favorable opportunity of doing their part, with the unfortunate result of making them feel that others had assumed the responsibility. The absence of a parish school can be justified only on the ground that the number of Catholic families in any particular section is not sufficient to make it possible. There may be small groups of children to instruct in three or four more localities, and the pastor will then have to arrange dates for each; meeting them in the public school after hours, if he is permitted the use of it—otherwise, in the home of one of his people. It goes without saying that as a first requisite for success these dates should be of regular occurrence, definite tasks being assigned as a preparation for each occasion. Should it happen that in some large sections of the parish territory there is but a single child of school age, the same obligation remains of making due provision for it. A very great tax upon the time and convenience of the pastor, it is true, a real burden, but nevertheless a burden there is no escaping. When a non-Catholic tells us he is thinking of embracing the faith, we give him our individual attention, setting aside hour after hour for him. Is there any reason why we should not do as much for one baptized in the Church? One soul is a diocese. A pastor for instance who presents for Confirmation a large class of children admirably instructed, and has given no heed to the individual child, here and there, who through distance, inconvenience, or indifference on the part of the parents, was not with the others at the hours of instruction, has forgotten the injunction "to leave the ninety-nine in the desert, and go after that which was lost until he find it."

St. Paul went so far as to say that he was sent not to baptize but to preach, and even thanked God that he had not baptized "any among you." We have all been ordained to the three-fold mission *docendi, regendi, benedicendi,* the latter including administration of the sacraments and sacramentals. Is there not often discoverable a tendency to practically centre all effort on this last one? Is it not possible that relatively it may absorb too much of our attention, with the result that the other two functions, and especially that of *docendi,* are to a great extent neglected? If our mission is, first of all, to make God known, a real passion for instructing the young, and a rare capacity for doing so, would seem an essential characteristic of the priestly vocation. Unfortunately there are many in the sacred ministry who give it little or no attention at all, and who show no inclination for the task. Perhaps I should have said they give it no attention because they have no inclination, and I might add they have no inclination because they are without the capacity to do it successfully. Almost without exception, it is often remarked, the school teacher who becomes a priest is most devoted to the work of catechizing. "As a matter of course," is the usual rejoinder. But what is the inference? That a very large proportion of pastors and assistants would be equally devoted with equal training in the art of doing it. In this as in everything else, all or nearly all have to be shown how. Just as few can qualify for a bookkeeper's position without having attended a business college, and just as few dare to allow their names on a program for a "reading" who have not had an elocution teacher, so it is too much to expect that the average person will conduct a catechism class successfully without some understanding of the scope of the work and of the methods to be adopted. All seminaries recognize the necessity of such a training in order to make a morning meditation or prepare a sermon; few seem to admit its usefulness to the catechist.

V

A priest's work is not finished so long as there are adults without sufficient instruction. There is no parish in the country or city without many. Whenever children are catechized in presence of the Sunday congregation, older members are heard to remark that their class need this as much as the children. For some the opportunities for religious instruction in childhood had been limited to a few weeks' drill preparatory to Confirmation; for others not even so much. If they and we are under no obligation to supplement this, if the Faith can be fervent and vigorous and practical on so frail a foundation, why compel our parish school children to give half an hour daily to religious study during a period of eight, ten, or twelve years?

The Encyclical of Pius X requires, in addition to the Gospel homily on Sunday morning, and in addition to the children's hour of catechism, a catechetical instruction for adults once a week, regu-

RURAL PASTOR'S WEEKDAY

larly announced and carried out. The country pastor who will undertake to bring this instruction within easy reach of all his people has before him a work of zeal not less arduous than commendable. To consider their convenience, at least to the extent of making his efforts effective, he may find it necessary to assemble them in different groups according to their place of residence. If he have two or more churches to attend, there seems no possibility of catering to all, short of a regular hour for this instruction in each church. In many parishes there are groups of families too far removed from any church to avail themselves frequently of such opportunities. They are likely also to be the souls most in need of this special attention. Little can be done for them if the pastor cannot make it convenient to assemble them for an hour of catechetical instruction in one of their homes. It is quite clear that under circumstances such as I am describing there can be no question of providing weekly instruction for all. The best possible is to give each congregation, or section of a congregation, its turn. We are trying to provide occupation for the pastor on whom idle hours hang heavy, and it is only fair to suggest that the turns of each congregation, or section of a congregation, be multiplied in proportion to the amount of time he is trying to fill in.

VI

The instruction of converts takes up a considerable portion of afternoons or evenings, and there are no parishes that lack converts to instruct. It was a quite frequent remark of the Venerable

SOME PASTOR'S PROBLEMS

Father Magnien that if the Apostles had devoted themselves only to the sanctification of those already within the fold, they would never have gone beyond Jerusalem and the Holy Land. The pastor of souls who has never helped others into the fold, who has never brought the light of Faith to those who were without it, has not completed his mission, no matter how long and faithful his service in administering the Sacraments and preaching the word of God.

In recent years we have been attending to the side of the work which gives little promise, and neglecting what would surely bring immense results. By means of missions, controversial literature, etc., we have endeavored to enlighten non-Catholics, to get them thinking, to convince a certain number. This was good. Meanwhile we neglected many who had no difficulties to remove, who were actually knocking at the door of the Church, and who with the necessary individual attention would joyfully have been admitted into her bosom. There are such people everywhere; they are within the reach of every pastor or assistant. They have heard God's voice calling them, and are only waiting for his minister to bring them home. Indisputable evidence is found in the fact that some priests are never without a class of catechumens, no matter how varied the conditions surrounding their appointment. This work is always going on. At the beginning of each year one is just as sure that a certain number of non-Catholics will come for instruction, as one is sure that a certain number of Catholics will come to confession within a given period. And the singular feature is there was apparently none to instruct in any of those parishes before his time, nor did the

RURAL PASTOR'S WEEKDAY

numbers continue long, after his removal therefrom. The real secret is, he attended scrupulously to everyone willing to be instructed, sparing neither time nor trouble; and most likely, when he had reason to hope that someone within his territory was wishing to consider the claims of Faith, he took the initiative, and proposed a course of instruction. In short, he had been faithful in a few things and was placed over many. To what extent would converts annually increase the Catholic population of North America, did every non-Catholic so disposed receive similar attention? Certainly by several tens of thousands. The rural pastor prepared to make the experiment will find many hours of interesting employment awaiting him. True, he will often be tied down when he would long to be free; nevertheless he also is contemplated in the commission: "Other sheep I have, that are not of this fold; them also I must bring, and they shall hear my voice."

Practically all that has been said of converts applies to another class who furnish the pastor continual interest and employment—adults who have never received the sacraments. If the type does not abound in numbers so large, it is none the less ubiquitous. Whether it be the neglected boy or girl of sixteen or seventeen, or the man in his sixties who faintly recalls a prayer repeated at his mother's knee, and much of the seamy side of life ever after, the regularity with which such persons report for instruction, and the simplicity and docility with which they accept every explanation of doctrine, afford repeated gratification. These statements are based on an experience furnished by intimate acquaintance with congregations in half a dozen city parishes, and an equal number of towns and country

SOME PASTOR'S PROBLEMS

districts. If some of those unfortunate delinquents did not become all we expected, the fault was ours. Every pastor and assistant with time at his disposal will find much to do in this sphere.

VII

Lastly there is the duty of regularly visiting parishioners in their homes. The statutes of at least one American diocese strictly require a quarterly visit to every family. A most thoroughly zealous pastor of my acquaintance assigns districts to his several assistants, and insists upon every family being visited monthly. There are parishes in English cities in which a weekly visit is made, at least to those families whose compliance with religious obligations is not perfectly regular.

No other form of activity so surely stamps a pastor as a man of real, unflagging zeal, whether in the opinion of the people he moves among, or of his coworkers in the ministry, or of his ecclesiastical superiors. Perhaps at no time in the history of Catholicity has this line of effort been so generally recommended as in our day. For some reason or other, however, it is a practice which does not appeal to the majority of priests. The courage necessary to answer call after call to the isolation hospital, or to districts where pestilence is raging, is never wanting; the energy and determination required to go from house to house, over and over again, seem often to fail. It is difficult to spend so much time and effort upon occupations from which few results are immediately and distinctly evident. "When a family is exemplary," one reasons, "what is accomplished by calling at their homes?" I am not at all sure of having the right answer to the question.

Holy Writ demands as a primary qualification of the good pastor that he know those that are his. The intimacy of the acquaintanceship desired is described by the parallel, "As the Father knoweth me and I know the Father." Something much more than a personal recognition is here suggested. He who would look after them and answer for their souls must understand their character, their habits, and the influences which enter into their lives, either to sanctify or to lead astray. At least as much is expected of him whose duty is to guide, whose advice is sought in matters of the greatest moment, whose word is so often law. "The sheep hear his voice: and he calleth his own sheep by name, and leadeth them out."

Nor is this all. There is the further requirement, "Mine know me." The youngest as well as the oldest feel at ease in the presence of the true pastor. All know him; all trust him. He has their confidences; there is no embarrassment, no reserve. To him they unburden their cares, they speak of their joys and hopes. But all this cannot be if they see him but rarely, if his visits are few, if he is a stranger, if because of this unfamiliarity his appearance intimidates rather than encourages. "He goeth before them, and the sheep follow him because they know his voice. But a *stranger* they follow not, but fly from him." Of all the tributes paid by a congregation to the memory of their departed pastor none gives so true a picture of earnest devotedness as that contained in the words, "Every home looked upon him as one of the family," or

SOME PASTOR'S PROBLEMS

in those other words, so expressive in their simplicity, "He would drop into the house at any time and we never minded it in the least."

We must not forget that it is by personal influence, not by logical argument or great learning, that the simple truths of the Gospel are propagated. A priest's power for good depends largely upon the esteem and love with which his people regard him. Not every priest can make himself a great preacher or a scholar; but no priest who associates freely with his people, dividing his time among all, is ever without their appreciation, or fails to gain their confidence. "My sheep hear my voice, and I know them, and they follow me." That priest alone is without influence among his people who does not choose to inspire it.

Just here I should like to bring a commonly accepted opinion into controversy. We often hear a priest's success accounted for in such remarks as this: "He knows how to take them"—"He has a way of getting along with them"—"He has rare tact"—"He is a real diplomat." Valuable as the man of the world may find such gifts, it is doubtful if they count for much in him who appears before the people as God's minister. His continued presence among them, his willingness to give them every attention consistent with his position, secures an ascendancy over their minds and hearts which no studied effort or cleverness of method can replace. Provided his words and conduct always evince the true priestly spirit with the ordinary traits of a gentleman, his parishioners are willingly blind to, or gladly forgetful of, other deficiences. There is practically no limit to the support a people will give the pastor who, through solicitude for their best interests,

RURAL PASTOR'S WEEKDAY

regularly visits them in their homes. I have never known such a pastor to be without an influence almost incredible, even in spite of many shortcomings. I have known many of intelligence and dignity and skill in the ways of the world who failed because of their aloofness.

This is only one reason out of many for visiting the members of the congregation. New sources of occupation are soon revealed. There are errors to correct, abuses to remedy, evils to forestall, misunderstandings to remove. There are the negligent to reform, the indifferent to arouse, the needy to assist, the discouraged and care-worn to cheer. There are good works to be promoted, good intentions to be approved, new practices to suggest and then to be furthered. The more faithfully the pastor attends to the multiplicity of duties, the more numerous and varied they become. Resources will not be wanting to him who goes about doing good.

Comparisons are sometimes made. How is it that one congregation in the midst of several gives numerous marks of fervor? How is it that its members assist at daily Mass and approach the sacraments so frequently, that they are faithful to every religious duty, and lead such exemplary lives? They themselves have no explanation to offer, but unquestionably and unconsciously they were following the lead of one who had lived and moved among them for years, and who, they always felt, was one of themselves. All those devout practices were suggested and repeatedly urged by one who was near and dear as a father, and no one could think of refusing what he knew was the pastor's wish. It is God's plan—and the very thought of

SOME PASTOR'S PROBLEMS

it must terrify us—that the distribution of His graces depends largely upon the will and the activity of His minister; that His children identify service of their Master with the wishes of him who is here to represent Him; and that their personal regard for that representative be always a force to remind them of Him and of their own eternal interests.

Some months ago contributors to the REVIEW discussed the use a priest could make of his spare time. One is tempted to ask the question: "Has a priest any spare time?"

CHAPTER VIII

THE COUNTRY PASTOR'S WEEKDAY

TO the paper on this subject in the last issue I should like to add three important considerations. In a rural district no small amount of a pastor's time may be taken through accommodating the hour of daily Mass to the greater advantage of his parishioners, zealous attention to the aged and permanently invalided, and affording the greatest possibilities for frequent confession.

A pastor's weekday Mass is primarily for his people, and not, as it would almost seem, a matter of private devotion. All should be encouraged to have part and take part in it, at least to some extent. In city churches its commencing punctually at the same hour daily may be the most effective means of promoting this devotion; in certain country congregations something almost the reverse of this may be necessary. To have made attendance possible for families in the adjoining village or for town people of leisure, in utter forgetfulness of all at some distance from the church, is accomplishing only the minimum. To say Mass every day in the parish church, and on Sunday only in a mission chapel which accommodates an outlying congregation, is to recognize but a very limited obligation toward that portion of the flock. To expect the children of the parish school or of the immediate neighborhood to assist at Mass daily, and to have this primarily in view in fixing the hour, is perhaps the greatest mistake of all. Few children will assist at Mass every morning with anything like becoming devotion. Of the adults whom we find frequently at weekday Mass, not one in a hundred, perhaps not one in a thousand, was brought to the practice by being obliged to appear there every morning during his school years.

The problem, then, of securing attendance at weekday Mass becomes largely one of distribution. Few will fail to respond, at least occasionally, when arrangements are made for their particular convenience and benefit; many will not make an effort once in the year on an indefinite appeal which to their hearing suggests little more than a sentiment of devotion and respect toward the Sacrifice of the Altar. It may be remarked in passing that, while we speak with enthusiastic admiration of the beautiful variety of the liturgical year, we proceed to present the weeks and days of that year in a wearisome and uninteresting monotony, concealing its teaching and attractiveness from the faithful, whose edification is the very purpose of its existence and preservation. It is well, therefore, to make something of the feasts that are not of obligation, announcing Mass at a later hour on those days. The Feasts of the Sacred Heart, Precious Blood, the Purification, Annunciation, Nativity, and Presentation of the B. V. M., the Apparition at Lourdes, the Commemoration of the Scapular, the Feasts of St. Joseph, St. Ann, St. John Baptist, Sts. Peter and Paul, etc. have a real interest for all well instructed Catholics. Most people are willing to make efforts in this direction during Advent and Lent, while any attention given to Rogation Days, All Souls' Day, the Feast of St. Blase, and other occasions of special devotion is sure to assemble large numbers.

Convenience in assisting at Mass depends also upon the occupation, circumstances, and respective distances from the church. This should be kept in mind even to the extent of announcing Mass at different hours on different days of the week, with the view of making provision for each class. In the case of school children within easy distance, some pastors have found that to require their attendance just one morning weekly gives the best results.

Most Catholic people, especially in country places, soon evince a willingness to be present at Requiem High Mass announced as month's mind or anniversary of a deceased friend or acquaintance. An occasional exhortation from the pulpit will be sufficient to promote this.

The above suggestions contemplate a pastor with only one church to attend. Where his care extends to two or more distinct congregations, there seems to be no reason why all should not receive equal consideration, as far as health and leisure permit. If thirty or forty or fifty families find themselves located at some distance from the parish rectory, that is not ample justification for cutting them off forever from the benefit of a weekday Mass. Being with them frequently under such conditions may entail considerable difficulty, but, on the other hand, their appreciation of any effort we make in this direction more than repays the time and trouble we give to it. In general it may be said that a prevailing indifference to opportunities of assisting at Holy Mass argues some radical defect in either people or pastor, if not in both.

Somehow or other, we get the impression that sick calls—adminstering the Sacraments in danger of death—represent a very considerable proportion of a priest's labors. How is it we hear so little of the time regularly required to attend the aged and invalid who are unable to receive the Sacraments in the church? Here is a duty much more extensive and burdensome than the other. Ordinarily more than one in every hundred of a parish population will belong to this class. To enable ten or twelve to receive the Sacraments monthly—as would be required in the congregation of a thousand souls—becomes an undertaking of some magnitude, especially in a country parish where the majority may live several miles away. I recall one zealous pastor whose congregation of over three thousand was made up of town residents and farmers from one to seven miles distant. Communion weekly for invalids within the town, and monthly for all outside, was the fixed rule, regular provision for which, his assistants understood, was no less essential than their presence in the confessional on Saturday afternoon and evening.

If we are really in earnest in the desire to promote frequent Communion, here is a portion of our people who cannot consistently be overlooked. Their condition craves our consideration; our visits will be among the few cheerful events in their sad, quiet lives; it will be our consolation to have done this great work of charity. Meanwhile their dispositions are assured. They are living lives of seclu-

RURAL PASTOR'S WEEKDAY

sion; they are no longer engrossed in worldly interests; their contemplations readily turn to God and eternity; their privations and sufferings lead them along the way which their Redeemer chose for Himself; where else outside the cloister shall we expect grace to fructify in greater abundance? As ministers of grace how can we refuse them generous attention?

It can be safely urged that multiplying opportunities for confessions, facilitating approach to this Sacrament, will necessarily contribute to its frequent reception. Let us not be afraid of "spoiling" our people in this way. Going to confession at all is a very decided effort, even for the fervent; why hesitate to relieve the burden? In the administration of city churches we commend the multiplication of confessors, promptness and patience in the discharge of their duty, and every other regulation calculated to remove the penitent's difficulties and inconveniences; why so great timidity in removing the obstacle of distance for the country resident, with whom going to confession means the expenditure of hours, providing a conveyance and frequently contending with unfavorable roads and weather? If circumstances do not permit multiplying churches for his convenience, what objection can there be to multiplying our visits in his neighborhood? Perhaps a careful scrutiny of conscience might reveal that the dread of trouble to ourselves much more than of injury to his spiritual interests controls our decision. It is sometimes said, "Give people the habit of going to confession near home and they will decline to go a distance." I wish to state emphatically that all my experience is in flat con-

SOME PASTOR'S PROBLEMS

tradiction of this. Make a more frequent confession possible for people and they will thereafter make greater sacrifices to maintain this frequency. Surely, the grace of this Sacrament attracts; surely their appreciation of that grace will become greater.

No matter what the conditions, every country pastor will wisely reserve all the hours after midday on Saturday for service in the confessional. His resourcefulness in adapting plans to particular exigencies and his generosity in carrying them out, will have practically all to do in securing frequent confession, and therefore frequent Communion, among his people. If his parish be compact, the process is simple, though he may find it advantageous at times to reserve certain hours for the convenience of those penitents whose circumstance of distance or occupation render attendance more difficult. If, on the contrary, a considerable number are remote, he should arrange to hear confessions during the afternoon in some house in that locality, leaving the evening hours for the accommodation of those who can easily get to the church. These remote groups of families may be settled in several localities in opposite directions from the rectory. This condition the pastor can meet by distributing the Saturday afternoons of the month among the different groups. A similar distribution of his time will ordinarily solve the problem of providing for the greatest number when he has two different churches to attend on Sunday. Outlying small missions are usually more or less scattered, and may necessitate his arranging an hour of confession in some private house, to provide better opportunities for one or other given sections. The young priest may think that he usually finds ample time on Sunday morning in small missions to hear the confessions of all who present themselves. Precisely; and the number of confessions will continue limited so long as he limits his people to this one opportunity. Multiplication of opportunities invariably leads to multiplication of confessions. In this great work of zeal it is for us to set the pace, not the people. The more a pastor contrives to have it generally understood that Saturday afternoon, and not Sunday morning, is the proper time for confessions, and the more he endeavors to realize this idea in practice, the better the results from every point of view.

A certain portion of the pastor's weekday leisure will be claimed by the delinquent. Every parish has its quota of these. In country districts where temptations against the Faith acquire little momentum, where the exemplary conduct of one's neighbor is a constant, living inspiration, where neglect of religious duties is rare, where negligence in their fulfilment brings disrepute and disgrace, such cases should be rare. Much of this may prevail in cities, despite the most energetic pastor's zeal; it will not assume grave dimensions in a country parish where the pastor does his part. Among the people we are accustomed to deal with on this side of the Atlantic, delinquencies are rarely accompanied with complete loss of faith. For this reason especially the hope of reform is much greater than is generally supposed. A young pastor will err in underestimating the power he possesses over those unfortunate fellows. The remedy is much less in tact than in a frequent visit, every care being taken to preserve Christian patience and a gentlemanly consideration. Ninety-five per cent, at the very least, will yield sooner or later. Even the most stubborn cannot fail to ap-

SOME PASTOR'S PROBLEMS

preciate the effort a priest is unselfishly making for their greater good, nor will God, on His part, fail to bless an effort inspired by the desire to gain Him another soul. But, on the other hand, no pastor with time at his disposal can justify neglecting to go again and again after those lost sheep of his fold. In studying the case of delinquents in country parishes, the question of marriage or no marriages becomes a live issue. It would seem that few men will continue faithful in the discharge of their religious duties without a mother, a sister, or a wife to lead them on.

CHAPTER IX

ATTENDING SCATTERED MISSIONS

HOWEVER much those of us whose native tongue is English may feel the need of a more extensive Catholic literature, we certainly cannot complain of the dearth of valuable works on the subject of Pastoral Theology. Already three Cardinals have left the stamp of their genius on treatises truly able and admirable; others, like the late Bishop Hedley and Father Keatinge, deserve our lasting gratitude; while the past twenty years have presented the interesting spectacle of fiction being wielded to serve the same purpose. All of these, however, contemplate the priest dealing with congregations in normal conditions. Not much has yet been said to guide him in difficulties which vary with the variety of circumstances under which an individual or group of individuals find themselves. For the purpose of drawing attention to some of these, the following suggestions are offered regarding the attending of a scattered mission, or one in which a small number of Catholic families are located for the most part at a considerable distance from the church and from one another.

The rule which most surely covers every requirement is that which says: "Their fervor will increase or decline in proportion to the time which the priest spends in their midst." It is the limitation to this time more than inexperience, or lack of training, or accomplishments, or tact, which stands out as the one impediment seriously affecting the spiritual care of such congregations. The young assistant, always ready for late and early hours in the confessional, for High Mass Sunday after Sunday, for the aftermidnight call to the Emergency Hospital, may very likely demur at the prospect of absenting himself frequently from his room or library or accustomed pursuits to pass hours and days with no pressing engagements, taking part perhaps in conversations and pastimes in which he finds no interest. Even the Indian missionary, deprived of every luxury, often of the commonest necessaries of life, subjected to all manner of hardships and fatigues, finds nothing more trying than the want of companionship, the dull, wearying routine, the frequent returns of ennui. All this, however, does not excuse us; we have been ordained for the people; our time is for them.

God has willed that the Grace on which their salvation depends come through our ministry, and, as Cardinal Newman has established, "Personal influence is the means of propagating the Truth." Herein lies our power over their minds and hearts. It is instinctive in a fervent Christian to crave for the recognition and affection of the priest. Much more than we generally imagine, they are given to identify their devotion to religion with the esteem in which they hold their pastor. Illogical, unwarranted, as his conduct may seem, that state of mind which makes it possible for a man of Faith to stay away from Mass because of some dislike for the priest is a consequence of this. And there is also the consoling feature that a very much larger number are corresponding more faithfully with their

SCATTERED MISSIONS

religious duties because of the personal regard they entertain for him. If, therefore, we would bring the people to God, we must be among them; if we would be all we should be in assisting them in their struggle for eternal happiness, we must be with them not only in spirit and affection but personally and actively. In a country mission how can those intimate relations exist between pastor and people if they see him only during the few hours he is in their church on an occasional Sunday morning?

Then, we must not forget that these people generally do their part; they contribute to our support without a murmur; they answer our call; they follow our lead; they are willing to give us their absolute confidence. No wonder they experience a feeling of abandonment, observing us month after month, year after year, without any disposition to be near them, or to cultivate their friendship, or even serve them beyond the minimum of time which the broadest conception of duty demands. Should this small distant congregation be residents of a town, our frequent visits become a matter of still more urgent need. There are greater temptations; there are more dangerous forces at work; there are greater distractions; there is less simplicity of Faith. Any neglect on our part may soon be attended with serious consequences.

There are other reasons demanding the prolonged stay in a scattered mission, and these more cogent than the former. Those people, like all others, must have ample opportunities of receiving the Sacraments; they also need instruction and exhortation; children are to be instructed and prepared for the Sacraments; adults in similar need will be found occasionally; sometimes there is a convert to in-

SOME PASTOR'S PROBLEMS

struct; there are delinquents to be aroused; the old and invalid to be attended; now and then an unfortunate marriage case to be adjusted; there are prevailing evils to be stamped out, scandals to be prevented, quarrels to be settled; there must be time for the care of the church and the sanctuary; from time to time acolytes are to be trained and every provision made that Holy Mass be offered with all the respect and reverence possible; in many places time and effort can maintain a choir capable of contributing to the devotion of the congregation. It goes without saying that in these days of rural telephone service, improved roads, and motor cars at a price which all can reach, failure to meet the needs of a scattered congregation is less easily excusable.

It is perfectly clear that all this can not be accomplished in a hurried trip on Sunday morning, leaving for home again as soon as the congregation has dispersed after Mass. Very often nothing more is possible just then because of the exigencies which oblige a priest to multiply himself on Sunday in order that the greatest possible number have an opportunity of hearing Mass. But when the Sunday rush is over, can we sit leisurely in our libraries satisfied in conscience that we have done all that can reasonably be expected of us in fulfilling our obligation toward the people at a distance?

Successful work among even a very limited number so circumstanced requires a more than ordinary initiative. There is a danger of our overlooking this. In a compact parish, no matter how large, the manifold ordinary duties easily adapt themselves to a routine. The hours for Mass, confession, etc., come round of their own accord; religious instruc-

SCATTERED MISSIONS

tion is conducted at fixed hours in the parish school; one hundred or two hundred are prepared for confirmation, no further organization being necessary than dividing them into a certain number of classes. There is little in the way of our administering a city parish much the same as a neighbor administers his. But in a scattered mission the distance of families from church and from one another, the inconveniences of seasons, road, etc., and the absence of Catholic schools necessitate a constant foresight in assembling people, or meeting them individually, so that the hearing of a few confessions, the preparing fifteen or twenty children for the Sacraments, is accomplished only through a succession of plans and appointments as varying as the circumstances to be provided for. The ceaseless demands on the time and energy of priests assigned to large city parishes have no parallel in the life of a pastor whose flock, though scattered, is not numerous.

Nevertheless a pastor so situated, proving himself equal to one emergency after the other, whose people give evidence of adequate attention and thorough training, leaves no doubt that success was due to a rare resourcefulness and a rare capacity for organization.

Edifying attendance at public devotions, varying with the recurrence of feasts and liturgical seasons, so characteristic of the fervent city parish, it is useless to attempt to secure in a country church, most of whose people reside at a considerable distance. The efforts of the zealous pastor who has to face such a condition must be confined in great measure to the promotion of devotions which may be practised in the home. There is also the compensation that the quiet of a country home affords greater facilities for private and family devotion than are possible amid the distractions of the busy, pleasure-seeking city.

Through his visits to the home as well as through the pulpit the practice of family prayer can be universally established. Devotions in accordance with the season can be provided for by recommending in addition, e. g. the use of meditations and reflections on the Passion during Lent, the Litany of St. Joseph in March, the Thirty-days' Prayer to the Blessed Virgin in May, the Litany of, or acts of Reparation to, the Sacred Heart in June, the Litany of the Saints on Rogation Days, the regularly prescribed Rosary Devotions in October, etc., etc. Providing homes with suitable and ample reading matter is the task easiest of all to accomplish. A little effort year after year makes the church library possible under the most straitened financial conditions. No district is too distant, no people are too scattered, to be honored by the visit of the Catholic book-agent, especially when assured of the pastor's coöperation. A like assistance will be guaranteed in prevailing upon parents to supply their houses with religious pictures, statues, crucifixes, etc., an object well worthy the zealous pastor's attention. Some managers of Catholic weeklies have already agreed, and probably all would agree, to the proposal that the paper be sent free of charge for three or four weeks to every family in the mission on the pastor's furnishing the names and addresses. With the usual exhortations from the pulpit on the duty of providing Catholic reading for the home, it has been found that an average of more than ninety per cent asked to continue the subscription when the three or four months had expired. I have dwelt

SCATTERED MISSIONS

on these details at some length, because we generally discover that people deprived of all the advantages of attending church regularly are precisely those whose homes are lacking in all those externals which contribute to private devotion, and because the pastor can succeed in having the families of a scattered mission so provided with these helps with no greater difficulty than will be required to place them in the homes of a city parish. When people can assist at Mass only once or twice a month, more than ordinary care is required on the part of the pastor to keep them mindful of the obligation of sanctifying Sunday. In every congregation so circumstanced we find certain good families scrupulous in the practice of setting apart an hour or more for reading the prayers at Mass, reciting the Rosary, teaching Catechism, or other pious exercises.

This we can safely teach and exhort. Whether in the pulpit, or the confessional or in private conversations, to lay this down as an invariable rule will produce none but the most wholesome results. The true Catholic home is well supplied with prayerbooks. The pastor will do well to interest himself in the character of the prayerbooks offered for use. Between the aim to catch the eye with an attractive, costly binding and the aim to produce a book occupying the least possible pocket space, publishers are flooding the market with a variety of manuals whose existence is probably impeding rather than stimulating the devotion of the faithful.

All these assistances can be provided for families in a scattered mission even more effectively than in a city. Not so with the work on which more depends than upon anything else—the instruction of the children. Here more than in any other undertaking will initiative be a desideratum in the pastor. It is claimed by some that the priest who finds no attraction and wins no success in teaching catechism is *ipso facto* disqualified for the work of the ministry. Whether such a one might do valuable service in a compact parish where the need is largely supplied by a parish school and religious teachers, he is certainly doomed to failure from the outset when his lot is cast among people deprived of these advantages. How are the poor children of the scattered congregation to be reached with anything like frequency? First and foremost, the pastor must impress upon parents in season and out of season that this duty is primarily theirs; that each house is constituted a school of religious instruction of which he will be the regular inspector. He can go further and teach parents publicly and privately how the work of this school should be conducted, how much—or rather how little—may be expected of the children each week and each month; he can point out the mistakes they as teachers are likely to make. When he has succeeded in having the parents attend to this duty under his direction, he will already have wrought wonders for the sanctification of the parents even more than of the children. Unless there reside in the vicinity an experienced teacher, zealous, devoted, and willing, it is better not to establish a Sunday School; it accomplishes little and parents will assume that they are thereby relieved from the obligation. Some pastors have the custom of confining their efforts to the six, or eight, weeks immediately preceding the date of First Communion and Confirmation, requiring the children to give most of their school hours to Catechism, perhaps requiring them to attend the

SCATTERED MISSIONS

parish school in town during that time. There is much to be said against the system; if a pastor dispenses himself from attending to the children's religious instruction during nine or ten months of the year, most likely parents will dispense themselves also.

Conditions in some places admit of a class being arranged for the Saturday evenings previous to the regular occasion for Mass. Failing this, and very often with it—because rarely can the more distant be got to attend—the practice of conducting a Catechism class in place of the ordinary Sunday sermons, the congregation still present, can be very safely recommended. Adult members always find it interesting and usually stand in need of it. Besides, a Catechism class well prepared for suggests admirable opportunities of here and there addressing oneself to the particular needs of adult members. How often educated men and women tell us that no sermon so appeals to them as the one given at the children's Mass. But since these occasions present themselves at best only once or twice a month, with distance, weather, roads, insufficient means of conveyance, and indifferent parents interfering, it will be absolutely necessary to arrange for hours of instruction on certain week days, varying the place of the meeting so that children of different sections may in turn enjoy the convenience afforded by shorter distance. Efforts such as these invariably meet with a generous response. At times one family, especially when isolated or when the parents are negligent, will require a special visit. No priest who has taken this trouble, assembling the children for Catechism round their own fireside, the parents present, absorbed and more or less conscience-

SOME PASTOR'S PROBLEMS

stricken, has ever regretted the expenditure of time it entailed. No warning so surely rouses parents to a sense of responsibility; it generally establishes a practice of home instruction and family devotions; even one visit has in some cases turned the members of the family, old and young, in the way of complete reform. We are reminded here also of a practice cited by one pastor to show how modern conveniences may be pressed into service of religious instruction. A family seven miles from church, no immediate Catholic neighbors, four or five children attending a public school, the father a Protestant, an easy-going Catholic mother who could not be trained to give any help—what was to be done? Once a week the pastor summoned the children one after another to the telephone, required them to state what portion of the Catechism they had severally committed to memory during the previous week; this he carefully noted down and assigned each a task for the following week. Then at his convenience, once in six or eight weeks, he visited the home to examine results and give such explanations of doctrine as time permitted. To carry out all these suggestions, it is evident, requires time, attention, and system; it is also evident that, these three requisites assured, no Catholic child need grow up uninstructed.

It must be remembered also that this is the day of frequent Communion and our obligation to promote the practice extends to both the distant and the near. We can succeed with the distant by always remembering the same three rules: Go often; Go early; Do not hurry back. Even in the most scattered congregations monthly confessions and Communion for all is a standard by no means too

SCATTERED MISSIONS

difficult to reach. In the last analysis it will depend on our readiness to minister to them. The priest in attendance can fix an hour for confessions on Saturday afternoon in some private house convenient to all in one quarter of the mission, thus leaving greater leisure on Sunday morning for people coming from other directions. In the statutes of some dioceses it is enjoined that the priest attending distant missions on Sunday remain for Mass Monday morning, thereby providing additional opportunities for approaching the Sacraments, especially for the aged and feeble. Then under certain conditions, in order to accommodate all, we shall have to fall back on the time-honored institution, so invariably associated with missionary experience and always recalled by the missionary with feelings of tenderness and consolation. I mean the *station*. Never do priest and people seem to unite in such genuine friendship, never does the awful reality of the priesthood dawn with such brilliancy upon the minds and hearts of those simple children of the Faith, as when, assembled in a small room at the command of His minister, they seem to hear the Son of God say as He did to Zacheus of old, "This day I must abide in thy house."

Associating, as is the universal practice of the Church, the public celebration of Holy Mass with the instruction of the congregation, I can suggest no more generous provision for Catholics enjoying so few advantages than by quoting the advice of one now nearing the completion of five decades in attendance upon scattered missions: "Never allow a congregation to go away without a few words of exhortation or explanation of doctrine. Whether it was a station, or funeral, or marriage, or some other happening, which brought them together, I could never resist an impulse which spoke in terms unmistakable, 'Have you, the ambassador of High Heaven, no message for those poor, struggling pilgrims?'" The very circumstances surrounding such situations are often an inspiration in themselves, and the priest speaks freely and warmly *ex abundantia cordis*. Nevertheless this must not be interpreted in support of the fallacy too often entertained that less preparation is necessary for a sermon to a small country congregation than for appearing in the cathedral of a large city. It is always the individual we are addressing; our communication is to him directly, not through the medium of the audience of which he forms a part; his intelligence is equally keen whether surrounded by fifty or by a thousand; our capability of impressing him is but slightly affected by his being alone, in the midst of a few, or in the midst of many hundreds. The older we all grow in the ministry the more willing we are to concede as a result of personal experience that any sermon of ours which commanded the people's attention in a country church or in a small town, was assured of a like success before a large city congregation; and vice versa, that any sermon which failed to reach the hearts of a city congregation would afford very little interest to the smallest country parish in the diocese.

Catholics who rarely if ever assist at Benediction, who never attend the Forty Hours' Adoration, in whose church the Blessed Sacrament is never reserved, may have only a very faint understanding of the doctrines of the Blessed Eucharist and the Sacrifice of the Altar, may be so little impressed by

SCATTERED MISSIONS

the astounding miracle of the Real Presence, as to go through life never entertaining the lively devotion which a realization of these truths should inspire. To arrange, *permissu Ordinarii,* a day of Exposition once a year in their little church would be a very slight tax on us and an experience of untold benefit to them. With the same object in view, we can also prepare to have the ceremonies of First Communion and Confirmation carried out with every possible effort at impressiveness.

The young priest unfamiliar with the situation may picture to himself an endless round of journeys as essential to living up to the suggestions offered in this paper. To combine these different tasks, to arrange that several, no matter how varying in character, may be attended to during each visit, is precisely the sphere in which his talent for organization will have play. A habit of looking ahead will be an invaluable asset, of thinking about things in time; then the effort of writing half a dozen postal cards or sending half a dozen telephone messages will generally make it possible to accomplish as much in one trip as otherwise would require days of travelling and trouble. But after all is said and done it must not be forgotten that the great essential factor of success in scattered missions is the priest's willingness to multiply his visits to them. There is nothing heroic in the undertaking unless in so far as a buggy or automobile ride now and then over country roads can be considered heroic. The bother of absenting oneself from home, the privation of comforts, wearisome delays, tedious hours in company not always interesting and congenial, all this also falls to the lot of any commercial traveller whose business takes him regularly away from the city. "And they to gain a corruptible crown, we indeed an incorruptible one."

There are many scattered missions of forty or fifty families where the Faith has been preserved for generations with a fervor rarely surpassed; to them city congregations are indebted for some of their most edifying members, and the priesthood and religious bodies for many valuable recruits. But when the total falls notably below forty or fifty families the outcome is decidedly problematic. An individual family living ten or fifteen miles from a church, a handful of Catholics scattered here and there, miles from everything, a prosperous town with four or five Catholic families and a church intended also to accommodate a few stray ones somewhere in the country around, an island on which half a dozen families have planted themselves, cut off from association with every other Catholic in the world—these are typical of conditions in which the most zealous pastor finds that little or nothing can be accomplished. His best efforts are largely in vain. The older people who have come there strong in the Faith will persevere; but what is there for the rising generation? They fraternize with non-Catholics, their surroundings are heretical, irreligious, worldly, pagan; mixed marriages will be the rule; the attendance of a priest is necessarily limited and the response more limited still. There is positively but one hope of saving their posterity to the Church—their removal from the place entirely. Preach this unceasingly; if possible, have a mission conducted among them with this as the avowed object; let every sermon aim at showing the absolute necessity of giving up their present surroundings if they would save their souls and the souls of their children and grandchildren. "Unless," you will say, "A man has his home there, his old haunts, his life-long friends, likely the grave of his parents or children; moreover his business is there, his position; the means of supporting his family. Can he be expected to forsake all this and go abroad after an uncertainty?" The obstacles are certainly great, but the attempt has been made more than once and with success. The results do not come all at once; but the ordinary Catholic warned of this, month after month, becomes afraid of the terrible responsibility he is assuming. He cannot go now, it is true, but he has decided that if, some day, he should have an opportunity to dispose of his business or property on reasonable terms or consider a prospect elsewhere, he will take advantage of it. Thenceforward he is *on the lookout;* he is in the state of mind which gives results—to be on the lookout; and some day the opportunity comes and he leaves.

Falling back on the old proverb which declares the relative values of prevention and cure, we might be tempted to ask: "Would it not be well if every congregation in the land were occasionally warned of the inevitable danger awaiting the children of those who would make a permanent residence in such places?" How many of us remember hearing this the theme of the Sunday sermon? How many of our Catholic papers emphasize, or even draw attention to, this danger?

I pray the reader not to be horrified at the final suggestion concerning these forlorn places, the towns and country districts with a population all but completely non-Catholic. Do not erect a church

SOME PASTOR'S PROBLEMS

there. It may be the cause of another family or two passing their days amid all those dangers to their eternal salvation. The average layman tempted by a business prospect, or an inviting salary, away from home, will inquire if the place possesses a Catholic church; assured of this he is satisfied and makes no further inquiries regarding the frequency of attendance, the provisions for religious instruction, what opportunities for weekday Mass, extraordinary devotions, etc., the number of resident Catholics, with whom his family may associate. By a mental process almost unconscious he assumes that the presence of a church is an encouragement for Catholics to locate there. Only months or years afterward does he fully realize what all this will mean. On the other hand the information that the place was without a Catholic Church would of itself have decided him from the outstart. The Catholic Church Extension Society erects small churches in districts unprovided for; occasions may arise when this seeming work of zeal could be a mistake.

CHAPTER X

WHAT IS THE OUTLOOK FOR THE GROWTH OF CATHOLICITY IN OUR CITIES?

THE press and legislative bodies of our country carry on the propaganda "Back to the Land." Beneath all this campaign is the assumption or rather the assurance that the manhood of a nation degenerates in city life. Little or nothing has been said as yet about the probable effect upon the faith and religion of the people who have spent years or generations as residents of a large and prosperous city. Indeed some of our zealous pastors maintain that the record of leakage in rural districts of this country, and the advantages the city offers in the possession of churches, schools, administration of the Sacraments, and all that goes to develop religious fervor and sentiment, justify the expenditure of effort in bringing our Catholic men from country districts to take up their residence in the city. Others on the contrary—most likely the majority—of our missionaries deplore the depletion of our country parishes. This article aims at supporting a theory that life in a large city *almost always tends to undermine the faith*.

We go so far as to say that *there are no city Catholics;* that a population of city Catholics left for three or four generations, without any recruits whatever from country districts, would certainly be in the last stages of irreligion and indifference; that for the most part the splendid examples of piety and practice which we witness in our city parishes, if examined one by one, will be found to be of people who either come from the country themselves or of the children of those who have come from country districts; and generally that the faith and piety of a Catholic residing or brought up in a large city are in proportion to the degree in which the country spirit has been operative in the home in which he was reared.

Before going further we wish to remind our readers, first, that all calculations on moral conditions have exceptions—"exceptions prove the rule"; and we therefore are prepared to hear of cases which would be exceptions to the above statement; secondly, we are speaking here of the *large* cities —that is to say, a city whose population is so great that the spirit which characterizes social life in the country and smaller towns is no longer found within it. Many of our smaller cities, of say ten, twenty, or thirty thousand inhabitants, perhaps more, resemble the country much more than the larger city in the unworldliness and quiet of their lives, in their freedom from dangerous influences and association, in the absence of distraction, sensation, and temptation, in the conditions which permit aspirations for another world to have place. The smaller towns and smaller cities hold the middle place between the country and large city in the possession of religious spirit, and—not absolutely, of course—but very much in proportion to the size of the given town or city. Thirdly, it should be said that, in order to arrive at a safe conclusion in matters of this kind it is necessary to study individual cases.

CITY CATHOLICS

We are quite prepared to hear that critics, highly reputable, characterize the theory here advanced as false, absurd. Why should they not? Can they not point to our Catholic American cities, to the splendid manifestations of faith therein, crowded churches at every service, the frequentation of the Sacraments, to the noble sacrifices our laity are making to support their churches and schools, and in contributing generously to every project undertaken, or even suggested, in the cause of religion? We realize that all this is true. Too much cannot be said in praise of the loyalty, generosity, obedience, and the reverence for their spiritual leaders to be found everywhere in our city parishes. But—and all we have to say turns on this question—*who are these splendid Catholics in our city parishes?*

The "we" in this article stands for the pastor and curates of a parish in a large American city, who for ten years carried on a systematic study of the effects on religion of life in the city and in the country respectively. The parish was small, always less than two thousand souls, a circumstance which gave us leisure to go fully into details. The results of our inquiry astounded us; every additional move, every new census served only to confirm the conclusions we were being driven to; so much so that at last we decided to give them to the Catholic public. Owing to the rapid growth of the city the population of the parish was constantly changing so that we had an entirely new population within the space of three years. Moreover, many of the newcomers were immigrants from different European countries, which gave the greater variety for the material we had to examine. We aimed at making the immediate acquaintance of every

SOME PASTOR'S PROBLEMS

newly arrived family or individual. In every case we asked the questions, "Where were you born and reared?" "Where were your father and mother reared?" We have kept an exact record of the census.

As in every other parish, there was a number of devout Catholics, and we found that these had themselves come from some country place or were the children of parents who had been brought up in a country place. It might surprise our readers to hear that during ten years of investigation we have only five or six cases on record of a faithful, devout adult Catholic both of whose parents were born and reared in a large city.

It was a regular practice for one of us to take note of who were the people present at weekday Mass, evening services, or any occasion of extraordinary devotion; almost always we found that every head of a family present was of country birth.

Within the walls of one class-room in any parish school, what a different promise of a future every pastor beholds in the character and conduct of the fifty or sixty children therein subjected to the same training! We found this the most interesting sphere of inquiry. The boy to whom the teacher would call our attention, dwelling upon his punctuality, his faultless behavior, his piety, we found invariably to be a child of parents not many years removed from their country home either in America or Europe. On the other hand the children of parents who had their own early training in the city—and that in many cases the very best any city could offer—just as surely fell far below the mark in all that was expected of a child brought up in a Catholic

CITY CATHOLICS

home, and trained in a Catholic school. We invite each and every pastor to take a census of his school population under these aspects.

In American cities it is a matter of frequent occurrence for a young man of city rearing to marry a girl brought up in the country and vice versa. We have found, after making the acquaintance of hundreds of such cases, that the religious spirit of the children is due to the parent of country rearing. One of the surprises we received in the early days of our inquiry was that of a husband exemplary in the practice of his religion whose wife could not even be got to attend Mass on Sunday. As time went on, the meeting of many such cases called for special examination of the causes. In the long list we have prepared there is not one exception to the rule; namely, the husband from the country, the wife a city product.

One census gives the following result:

Total number of married women in the parish 356
Women of country rearing 255
Women of city rearing 101
Of the 255 reared in the country 4 missed Mass habitually.
Of the 101 reared in the city 47 missed Mass habitually.

A census taken six years later gives the following:

Total number of married women in the parish 391
Women of country rearing 268
Women of city rearing 123
Of those 268 from the country 9 missed Mass habitually.
Of those 123 from the city 52 missed Mass habitually.

During a mission one year we recorded the minutest details of attendance during the men's week. Following are some of the statistics:

SOME PASTOR'S PROBLEMS

Total number of married men in the parish 286
Married men who failed to make the mission 89
Married men of country birth who failed to make the mission 4

Much evidence was gathered on this subject from our experience with the ordinary church societies. In these also we took statistics regularly and the result of all those inquiries could be best summed up in a challenge that would take this form: "We defy any pastor to keep a young ladies' Sodality or a Holy Name Society in existence for two years in a parish entirely composed of city people."

A very common objection we have heard made when announcing our conclusions is that America, being a young country, its cities must necessarily be made up of country people, or their immediate descendants. To this we have certainly found an answer in dealing with a large number of immigrants who have taken up their residence in our city and in our own parish. A young priest beginning his observations will be disappointed over and over again at the large number of people with Irish names whose faith and religious fervor fall so far short of the glorious traditions of their race. Soon afterward he will notice that the Murphy's and Healy's and O'Brien's and Casey's who do not go to Mass are not from Ireland but from England, and they will declare that their grandfathers and perhaps their fathers in Ireland would have sacrificed all the world had to offer rather than be disloyal to the call of religion. How is this terrible falling-off to be explained? We have only to remember that no Irishman ever went to England to engage in farm labor. They sought a livelihood in the industries of Liverpool or Manchester or

CITY CATHOLICS

Birmingham; they gave the first impetus to Catholicity in those cities; they died in the fervor of their faith and their grandchildren have sunk into indifference. Every pastor deplores the religious indifference of Catholics of Irish names who come from England. It is not the difference between Ireland and England, but the difference of country and city.

Of late years we have seen much of the professional tramp, who comes to our door for a meal or an order for a night's lodging. He gives his name, which is Irish, as are also his appearance and accent; he professes to be a Catholic; he is nothing else; generally he is ready to admit his dissipation; that it is years since he approached the Sacraments; that he never, or scarcely ever, goes to Mass. We always inquire about his early history, and our long list records only two of these unfortunates who claimed a country district as their place of birth. Meanwhile the column under this heading in the register has to its credit Dublin, Glasgow, London, Liverpool, New York, Boston, Philadelphia, Montreal, etc., etc.

Any one who goes into this question with any degree of thoroughness will probably revise his views as to the causes of mixed marriages. We are all considerably alarmed at the growth of this evil, especially in our large cities. We are all offering explanations of it; sometimes we blame the schools, or perhaps we think we have discovered a remedy by greater efforts on the social side of parish work. It is well worth while inquiring, case after case, who is this Catholic proposing to enter into a mixed marriage. All who inquire will be convinced of the prominent part which city life is taking in propagating this evil. If there be any young people in a city population who should have a reasonable excuse for seeking such dispensations it would surely be those who are practically strangers in the city, who have come recently from rural districts and have had little or no opportunity of making the acquaintance of Catholics. Still we find that among such Catholics mixed marriages are rare. It is the young men and women in the old Catholic families of the cities who are contracting mixed marriages. They and their parents were born and reared in the city; from their earliest years they had every opportunity of forming Catholic associations —perhaps they have done so—but two generations of city life has so damped the ardor of their faith that they feel no aversion to such unions.

Where do our priests and religious come from? Much of the best blood of the nation finds its way to the city; the children of such parents should give every promise of what is best; no city is without Catholic schools; city children of both sexes are constantly under the care of Religious; they have every advantage of religious instruction, of frequentation of the Sacraments, of every form of religious exercise; colleges and academies are at their door. From such children we should hope to recruit our clergy and our religious communities; and we are always lamentably disappointed. From such surroundings a few vocations are developed, but the great majority must always come from country places. We speak of New York, for instance, as a great Catholic city; but in that Archdiocese what a small proportion of a sufficiently numerous clergy ever has been made up of New York boys of the second generation! We should

CITY CATHOLICS

recommend each of our readers to ask himself this question: "Do I know one priest whose father and mother both were born and reared in a large city?" We think there must be such, but after ten years' inquiry in every quarter we have never heard of one. A similar inquiry conducted during the same length of time in regard to religious produced just one exception to the rule: a father and mother born in Glasgow whose three daughters are now in the cloister.

Thus it was that the statistics gathered from every aspect of this question pointed to the same conclusion. Month after month, and year after year, new incidents presented themselves to confirm suspicions which had been gradually rising. The conclusions we have come to sound like the views of an extremist. Nevertheless we are convinced that any one who will examine the facts before him in his own parish or among his immediate acquaintances will discover something precisely similar to what we have described. The alarming feature of it all is this: that no family leaves the country without *certain* danger to the faith of posterity. It is not a matter of chance where some improve and some deteriorate. There is no class of people, no system of training, no conditions of life, which seem proof against this usual result. No matter how fervent be the father and mother who take up their abode in a large city, their grandchildren or at the very furthest their great-grandchildren will give a very marked evidence of decadence of faith and religious practice. The only possible check on their speedy destruction will be in cases where their children or grandchildren choose people of country training for their life partners.

SOME PASTOR'S PROBLEMS

Now, if all this be true, have we priests any greater work of zeal than that of keeping our Catholic people in country districts? Have we any greater evil to contend with than the tendency at this moment of so many people of all classes to rush to the city? We are armed against what we call the great evils of modern times, alcoholism, Socialism, divorce, the public school, mixed marriage, race suicide, degeneracy of the poorer classes. Our pulpits ring with denunciations of these evils; our Catholic press expends its best energies in warning our people of these dangers; we organize to combat them. It hardly occurs to us that it is only our city Catholics who have anything to fear from them. Not even one of these dangers threatens the population of a country parish, nor do we seem to realize that urging a Catholic to exchange the country for the city is landing the poor fellow face to face with all these dangers. On the other hand most of us have exerted considerable zeal in what has had for effect nothing less than bringing our good Catholic people to the city. We have urged parents in the country "to do something for their boys," which simply meant giving them an advanced education that they might be one day prominent in a profession, or in business, or in politics and thus getting them off the farm. We have busied ourselves in securing positions in the city for them; perhaps we have even rejoiced to see our town or city parishes building up at the expense of a country mission and given some encouragement thereto.

Our readers who have followed us so far may justly remark: "Well, in any case there is nothing new in this matter; the whole question must be as

CITY CATHOLICS

old as cities." To the consideration of this we have given some attention. All three of us have spent years in Europe and during recent visits have been giving special attention to this question. We take the liberty of adding some of the facts collected.

In France, in the cities of Lyons and Bordeaux less than one-third of the Catholics go to Mass on Sunday; in Marseilles less than one-fifth. One of the staff relates that he and half a dozen visiting priests during a stay in Geneva were unanimous in their admiration of the Catholicity they witnessed in the parish of Notre Dame in that city: large crowds at Mass and at the Sacraments, etc., etc. From the pastor they eventually learned that the parish contained fifteen thousand souls, less than three thousand of whom were practical Catholics.

In Naples, the attendance is somewhat better, most likely due to the fact that Naples, being an industrial city, offers a constant inducement for country people to seek employment there. The churches of Florence and Venice, which cities have no positions to offer the farm laborer and are living on their past, present spectacles on weekday and Sunday distressing to the eye of a Catholic.

One spent four months among the country parishes of Bavaria and asserts that nowhere outside of Ireland has he witnessed such splendid manifestations of faith. What was his horror on visiting its capital—the so-called Catholic city of Munich—to observe that only a moiety of its men attended Mass on Sunday, and to learn that all its representatives in the Reichstag were Socialists. It may be interesting to add also that the country districts of Bavaria elect not even one Socialist.

Even in Catholic Belgium no traveller fails to

SOME PASTOR'S PROBLEMS

remark the sad contrast between the worldly, irreligious spirit of Brussels and the fervent simplicity of Flemish peasants. The historic town of Bruges, surrounded by the most fervent of Belgian peasantry, has three classes of inhabitants: the nobility, the prosperous commercial and working people, and the pauper element. All are supposed to be Catholic; those of the second class are practical Catholics; the nobility have lost their faith; to an inquiry whether or not the paupers of the slum districts went to Mass on Sunday the answer was: "Yes, *because* in this city the churches have charge of distributing the bread and clothing of charity." All these poor as well as the nobility are the descendents of the families of Bruges in the days of her glory; the second class represent newcomers from the surrounding country.

None of the examples we have just cited from abroad, however, fully establishes the theory we commenced to prove: that life in a city tends to undermine the faith of *all* its inhabitants. The particular specimen which we were anxious to examine was a city whose population had continued for generations without any intermingling of the blood of the peasantry. Perhaps the nearest approach to such is the Roman Trastevere. Here is a people who boast of their exclusiveness, who claim to be descendants of the old Romans of classic days and have refused to intermarry even with Romans at the other side of the Tiber. From the days of Constantine the Trastevere was supposed to be Catholic; its residents have ever had all the advantages of numerous churches and schools and the attendance of priests, religious, and saints. Still at this moment the new public school near St. Cecilia's has

CITY CATHOLICS

an attendance of fifteen hundred children who never go to Mass on Sunday and a free Catholic school in the same block, conducted by the Sisters of St. Vincent de Paul, with great difficulty secures a meagre attendance of one hundred and thirty. The traveller has only to see the congregation—or rather the almost complete absence of a congregation—in St. Cecilia's any Sunday to understand the awful religious indifference of the people.

The modern Venice is also an example of a city whose population for generations has received very few recruits from country districts. It also is an example of a city which for centuries has been favored with almost every advantage the Church can provide for her children. The magnificence of her numerous churches all the world speaks of; Catholic institutions of every kind abound; she has never known the privation of a learned clergy; religious communities devoted to the education of her youth and to every work of charity confront us at every turn. In her treasures of art which even her humblest citizen daily gazes upon—because they are everywhere—she possesses a means of Christian training such as no other people on earth ever have enjoyed. While provided with all these extraordinary means of grace she is even up to this hour free from almost all the evils which we are accustomed to look upon as the unconquerable enemies of religion. Venice was a Catholic state and fostered the development of religion; its laws as well as its schools, even to-day, interfere in no way with Catholic practice; the people have Catholic associations only; mixed marriage is unknown; divorce has never taken root in Venice; even Socialism has so far gained so little ground as to be unable to elect there

SOME PASTOR'S PROBLEMS

a single representative to Parliament. Notwithstanding all these conditions so favorable to the preservation of Catholicity, only a fraction of its population go to Mass on Sunday. What is the explanation? We know of no other unless that it is a city.

In the heart of London, in the city of Westminster, there is a community of Irish Catholics; there they have lived for several generations in an isolation that is possible only in a great city. Their district is within the limits of the Cathedral parish, though the attendant at Mass in the beautiful Westminster edifice sees nothing of them. A prominent member of the St. Vincent de Paul Society remarked: "We give them constant assistance, and sisters and priests visit them regularly hoping that through the continuous generous attention they will call for a priest at the hour of death." Still the reader has not to be informed that their ancestry a century ago in their humble homes in Ireland dreamed not that any one calling himself a Catholic could neglect his religious duties.

Lastly, what of Dublin? Dublin, the fervor of whose religious spirit no one surely doubts; and no wonder, for the traveller in Dublin with all he has preconceived of Irish faith and practice never expects to witness such congregations as every day and every hour swarm the churches of Ireland's capital. "Who can say," he exclaims, "that faith will not thrive in a city?" And we must confess that during our first days in Dublin we almost hoped that an exception could be found to our theory. As usual we set to work to inquire: "Who are these good people?" and again we learned that the backbone of every congregation of Dublin was made up

CITY CATHOLICS

of a class who, if they themselves had not come from the country, their parents had. One pastor remarked: "Cut off the immigration from country districts to this city for twenty-five years and our churches would be empty." Dublin, as every one knows, has numerous priests, diocesan and regular; it has large communities of religious, men and women; we found on inquiry that all these had to be recruited with subjects from country districts, the city not supplying one-third of the number required for its needs. This in a land that has sent apostles to every quarter of the globe! Something sadder still; Dublin has its Catholics who do not practise their religion. One pastor there stood authority for the statement that every year over a thousand fathers and mothers in poverty and degradation sell their children to proselytes. We visited the slum districts, mostly in the neighborhood of the Four Courts and Church Street; every traveller bears evidence to the misery and degeneracy that has taken possession of that unfortunate population. We went so far as to accost individual men and women, one after another, and inquire about their parentage. In thirty-nine cases out of forty-two they and their fathers and mothers were born in Dublin.

The Irish clergy throughout the country are doing everything in their power to prevent emigration, the reason being that so many who left home in the fervent practice of religion lost their faith in America. We took the liberty of saying to them: "Is it because they went to America or because in America they located themselves in cities?" Archbishop Hughes stated in 1852 that the Catholic population of New York City at that date was two hundred thousand. It would be interesting to know

SOME PASTOR'S PROBLEMS

how many of their descendants are practical Catholics to-day. Darcy McGee almost half a century ago made the statement that taking account of the number of Irish Catholics who up to that time had come to the United States and allowing for the natural increase, only one-third would be found practising their religion. There are evidently conditions near home that we should do well to examine.

The above presents, in a general way, some of the information we have gathered on this very extensive subject. To describe in detail the hundreds of individual cases which have come under our observation would be to furnish matters for a statistical report instead of an article in a monthly review. Nevertheless, it is this close observation of a multitude of individual facts that brings unwavering conviction. We cannot expect our readers to be as convinced as we are of the reliability of the theory we have advanced. We should gladly hear of substantial proofs to the contrary, for we shudder to think of the conclusions into which we have been forced. If what we maintain is true, what is to be the future of our own country, whose Catholic population is mostly to be found in the large cities? What of the tide of emigration, millions of Catholic people leaving their simple rural surroundings in Ireland or Poland or Italy or Malta, and condemning their posterity, within a few generations, to loss of faith in an American city? What of the good Catholic families lately arrived from country districts here, and at present the very life of our city parishes and the consolation of their pastors? Are their grandchildren, or at most great-grandchildren, to have all wandered from the fold? Gladly, therefore, would we find that we are wrong. But we

CITY LIFE

claim that no decisive answer can be reached on this question by observing Catholic congregations or Catholic populations in the mass. We must know the religious history of one member after another in order to understand of what that mass is composed. The growth or decay of faith, as all admit, is not a matter of one's own lifetime; and most of us are indebted to our grandparents and great-great-grandparents for whatever solidity of religious sentiment we possess. The investigation must be carried on by the study of the individual case. And only the priest who has leisure to be intimately acquainted with his people is in a position to carry on such an investigation. If there be any who regularly take a census of their parish, inquiring not only into the religious practice of the individual or the family, but also their place of birth, and the place of birth of their parents, we should be most interested in hearing the result.

CHAPTER XI

CATHOLICITY AND CITY LIFE

TO the Editor, *The Ecclesiastical Review*.

An article which appeared in the *Review* some months ago has no doubt been the subject of considerable discussion among your clerical readers. The awful conclusions suggested by the author could not but create a sensation, all the more alarming because, apparently, none of us ever suspected that such a condition of things could prevail in our very midst. The theory, it would seem, is nothing less than this. A young couple from the country, devout, exemplary, commence their married life in a large city. Their children, after enjoying all the advantages of church, parish school, etc., in due time choose as life-partners Catholic young men and women with precisely the same history. The offspring of these unions—this second generation of city-born Catholics—may probably remain practical Catholics, but in fervor they shall have fallen notably behind their grandfathers and grandmothers; while a priest or a religious from among such will be an incident of the very rarest occurrence. Now suppose this second generation of city-born Catholics should marry young men and women who are also of the second city-born generation, the offspring

Note. The author takes the liberty of inserting a comment by "Spectator" on the matter of Chapter X.

CITY LIFE

will, as adults, appear so devoid of faith and religious practice as to be no longer looked upon as children of the Church.

In view of the fact that from all parts of the world immense numbers of devout Catholics are crowding into large cities, the mere possibility of such an outcome is sufficient to rouse the keenest interest of all concerned. I must confess that upon reading the article for the first time I regarded it as rank absurdity, as foolish hobby-riding, and gave it no further attention. Of course, the natural process of refutation was to produce a list of cases whose history was in flat contradiction of the description given above; I did not know of any, but was quite sure that many could be found in every city.

My sense of security was first discomfited by a statement in the *Columbiad* of April, 1915, to this effect: "Dr. Dazso of Budapest says the fourth generation of city-dwellers is unknown." Shortly afterward this statement was repeated in presence of some priests from England, who replied, "It is generally maintained that this is the case in London." If either of those generalizations be well founded, if it be really so that the millions of Catholic families flocking to our cities these days will have left no posterity in a little more than a hundred years from now, then certainly there is ample reason for our making every effort to keep good Catholic people in the country. Father Graham assures us, however, that "there is a goodly number of Catholics here [Baltimore] whose parents and grandparents and great-grandparents—and beyond —were born and raised right here." This information to be applicable to the theory proposed by

Sacerdos would mean that in Baltimore there are many devout, faithful Catholics who with both their parents, their four grandparents and their eight great-grandparents were born and reared in that city. A list of people answering this description exactly would be of extreme interest to actuaries and statisticians. Would Father Graham have any objection to furnishing it?

What really stimulated me to further inquiries on this subject was the rather unsatisfactory character of criticism which the original article elicited. Taken in general, these criticisms were marked by three prominent features:

1. A frank admission of having no information to offer, although it was precisely this that the author of the article and the editor of the *Review* appealed to readers to furnish;

2. An assumption that the anonymous Sacerdos was a hobbyist and shaped his statistics accordingly;

3. The charge on *a priori* grounds that the theory "impugned the divinity of the Church" and even "bordered upon heresy."

The first and second of these need no further comment; the third deserves serious examination. Is it refusing to recognize the power of Grace to maintain that certain given influences will almost certainly undermine one's faith? Does one doubt the divinity of the Church who fears for the perseverance of one of her children already fallen among dangerous associations? Let us suppose that the Written Word had never contained the terrible sentence of our Lord, "How hardly shall they that have riches enter into the kingdom of heaven," and let us suppose also that some expe-

CITY LIFE

rienced pastor of maturer years emphasised that very idea as a result of his own observations; would not many of our devoted clergy protest that such a remark "ignored the efficacy of grace," "impugned the divinity of the Church," and therefore "bordered upon heresy?"

Not being connected with a city parish, I was obliged to await an opportunity of gaining information first-hand by my own personal efforts. Meanwhile I commenced discussing the question with fellow clergymen, from any and every quarter, with whom I was privileged to hold a conversation. That large number who were disposed to say "impossible," "absurd," "nonsense," I was accustomed to answer by proposing the following questions:

1. How many priests do you know of, who with their parents were born and reared in a large city or cities?

2. How many religious do you know of who as well as their parents were born and reared in a large city?

3. How many exemplary families of adult age do you know of who as well as their parents were born and reared in a large city or cities?

It is surely significant that as a result of this inquiry carried on for over a year the only case recalled was that of a priest who with his parents was born and reared in Greater New York. This, of course, does not demonstrate the non-existence of such cases even in the very parishes administered by the priests interrogated (since very few pay any attention to those circumstances at all), but it does go to show that those pastors are not in a position to dismiss with the pronouncement "preposterous,"

SOME PASTOR'S PROBLEMS

"rank nonsense," the claims of three members of a parish staff who tell us they gave ten years to an exhaustive inquiry into the details of the question.

Repeated discussion furnished considerable information bearing more or less directly on the subject and ordinarily not taken much account of. Allow me here to subjoin some of this evidence. A pastor in an Eastern city told me that not more than half his people attended Mass on Sunday. The pastor in one of our large Western cities was ready to admit that half of the married women of his congregation missed Mass habitually. A pastor in a city of over three hundred thousand souls in the middle West volunteered the information that his parish contained 1900 families of whom 700 families were practical Catholics. The large percentage of indifferent and fallen-away Catholics in the Southern States, the small Sunday congregations so disappointing to a traveller in the South, are commonly accounted for by the dearth of priests in earlier years, the people being so widely scattered as to make it impossible for missionaries to reach them. This, however, does not explain the coldness and indifference prevailing so extensively among those who profess to be Catholics in the *cities* of the South. A prominent pastor from one of those cities made this remark: "The South has little or no immigration; in the North Catholicity is being constantly recruited from the country districts of old lands; our newcomers are mostly from the North, and our Catholic recruits, therefore, are mostly from Northern cities." Augustinus in the March issue of the *Fortnightly Review,* speaking on the question of Catholic leakage, says: "The statistics given by Father Muntsch show that in England and Wales

CITY LIFE

more than a million souls have drifted away from the Church. The situation is no better, nay it is undoubtedly worse, in this country. Only a short time ago Judge D—— of the Chicago Boys' Court, assured me that ten thousand delinquent boys are hailed before this tribunal annually and that seventy-one per cent of them are of Catholic parentage. I verified the statement for myself by speaking to many of the boys in the court-room as well as in the lock-up. Most of them frankly admitted they were Catholic, but had neglected church and the Sacraments for years. A curate in an Eastern city of approximately six hundred thousand inhabitants told me he could hardly find a house in the parish without one or more apostates. We have been accustomed to glory in our real and imaginary perfections and to shut our eyes to defects. We have followed the advice of the professional "booster"; "Sell your hammer and buy a horn."

Most American priests have something to say about Catholic immigrants. All bear witness to the fervor and faithfulness which characterize the great majority of those who come from Ireland, Poland, Ruthenia, Bavaria, and the Rhine provinces —that is to say, from districts where agriculture is almost the exclusive occupation. What European cities have the reputation among us of contributing large numbers of immigrants remarkable for the staunchness and fervor of their Catholicity? Evidently none.

If it is really so, that one rarely meets an adult family of exemplary, devout Catholics (a family of at least four or five sons and daughters) who with their parents were born and reared in a large city, or cities, or if such cases are comparatively few in number; if it is uncommonly rare to find an exemplary family of adult Catholics whose grandparents, as well as parents, are of city rearing, it would be well to remember that practically every country parish properly attended can point to an exemplary population whose ancestry on every side have been country residents for generations incalculable.

Whatever large cities may claim to accomplish in preserving the faith among the laity, even a very limited inquiry leaves no doubt whatever regarding our dependence on country training for the necessary supply of sacerdotal and religious vocations. Since reading the article by Sacerdos, I have visited eight communities of women with the express purpose of asking the question, "How many religious have you who with their parents were born and reared in large cities?" Not being prepared for the question, their answer came later, and always to the same effect—"We do not know of any."

The large number of seminary students from the State of Iowa (whose Catholic population is largely rural) is in marked contrast with the alarmingly small number furnished by our cities possessed of immense Catholic populations. Every diocese devoid of a goodly number of country parishes is experiencing untold difficulties in this matter. That Brooklyn seminary no longer allows its students to spend the summer vacation with their families is probably a demonstration of this difficulty. A distinguished member of the Papal foreign service once told me that he was born in Rome, entered a boarding school of the city at the age of seven, donned the clerical dress, as is the custom, and was never once in his father's house until after his

CITY LIFE

ordination. Is it not very likely that this regulation, adopted, more or less generally, in some European countries, had its origin in dioceses which had to depend on city boys to recruit the priesthood? In any case it is not the practice in Ireland or in several other countries where the livelihood of the majority of Catholics is obtained from the land. One American bishop told me that his diocesan seminary was practically filled with native students of Bohemian and Polish extraction, while he had given up all hope of securing any English-speaking candidates from within his territory; all this notwithstanding the fact that two-thirds of the parishes of the diocese were English-speaking. The explanation is that the English-speaking parishes are in the cities and towns; while numerous colonies of Bohemian and Polish families are settled on the land. The most thoroughly Catholic city north of the Mexican line is certainly Montreal; nevertheless a Canadian bishop assured me that, if the archdiocese did not comprise an extensive country district, not more than one-third of the city parishes would be staffed. On the other hand, the diocese of Charlottetown in Canada, from an English-speaking population of 40,000, almost entirely rural, after equipping itself and manning a very prosperous college, has more than forty priests in active service in the United States and is supplying the greater part of the English-speaking priests, now in constant demand, in the Canadian Northwest. From the same territory almost every religious community of women in the Western States and in the Canadian West is securing postulants in goodly numbers. A story much the same is told by Canadian bishops in reference to the dioceses of Antigonish and St. John's,

Newfoundland, in both of which city life is practically unknown.

A question arises here. The church, the school, and the home are the three institutions which assume the responsibility of fostering a religious spirit and preserving the faith among Catholic peoples. It is tolerably certain that the city does not and cannot provide priests and religious to perform the part assigned to churches and schools: does the city, or can the city provide in anything but limited numbers parents capable of conducting an ideal Christian home? The universal complaint of city pastors is the deplorable lack of home training and guardianship, so great that priests and teachers are obliged to attempt the fulfilment of important duties which parents constantly neglect. At the same time we seem to be unanimous in the conviction that united efforts of church and school cannot make up for the training neglected in the home. If therefore the city must look to country districts for a supply of priests and for the religious who are to conduct the parish schools, academies, and colleges, *a fortiori* must it look to the country to supply in great measure the character of parents capable of inspiring a thorough religious spirit in the home.

An extended summer vacation, at length, provided the long looked-for opportunity of inquiry regarding the *individual* members of some city parish. Visiting the rector of a cathedral whose assistants were engaged taking a census, I begged the privilege of canvassing a district. With a few additional columns in the census note-book three weeks were spent going from door to door, and, without any hint being given of the purpose in view, each evening the rector was requested to pro-

CITY LIFE

nounce as "good," "bad," or "indifferent," the several families visited during the day. Of the families rated "good," which constituted more than two-thirds of the congregation, by far the greater number of parents had spent their childhood in country parishes or country towns; a considerable number had been city residents all their lives; not one case was found in which both parents, as well as their parents in turn, were of city rearing. The class denominated "indifferent" furnished histories almost as varied as the individuals composing it; country, city, town, each had made its contribution, while mixed marriages, orphanages, years spent where church attendance was impossible, with the consequent privation of religious instruction, were everywhere in evidence as undermining influences. Thirteen families were branded as "bad" or "hopeless." In one case both parents were from the country; in another both parents were from a town; in two others the fathers were from the country, the mother from the city; in nine both parents were of city rearing.

Some weeks later a small city parish became permanently vacated through the illness of the pastor. At the time the diocese was straitened to meet the people's needs, and I yielded to the bishop's request and spent the remainder of the summer there. The engagement has made it possible to learn the history of sixty-nine families. Six, while professing Catholicity, are to all intents and purposes lost to the faith. Dublin, Edinburgh, Manchester, two American cities, and a lengthy residence in the West, far removed from Church and Catholic associations, divide the responsibility. Some who are practical and attentive owe their allegiance to cities this side of the Atlantic; a few others speak of schooldays spent in European cities. But the solidly devout and exemplary, the real pillars of the church, father and mother alike, have come from country parishes. Up to the present I have not met among the regular attendants any case in which the father or mother as well as their parents grew up in a large city or cities.

The details I have furnished in this article are probably wearying: I have come to think this question is deserving of minute examination.

SPECTATOR.

CHAPTER XII

How Our Clergy Are Recruited

AT a recent clerical gathering, one of the number proposed this rather extraordinary question, "How is it that parishes with schools conducted by religious teachers furnish few or no candidates for the priesthood?" The protest almost universal which arose, as it were instinctively, was met by a review of the situation in our own diocese, the facts adduced being in almost perfect accord with the first speaker's contention. Various attempts to explain the paradox were then forthcoming, each in turn falling to the ground, as instance after instance was cited in flat contradiction of the theory advanced, until at length a voice from down the table suggested: "The whole matter is perfectly clear. Parochial schools and religious teachers are mostly in the cities and larger towns of the dioceses. We need never expect to recruit our ranks from those sources." Another citation of cases followed; such contrasts as that of a country parish of only four hundred souls, with no parish school, having thirteen priests in actual service in the diocese, and city parishes of four thousand souls but having no native priests, seemed to lend some confirmation to the view. One remarkable piece of evidence was of a city pastor, well known to all present and known as a man truly zealous in everything, who had made every conceivable sacrifice to foster vocations to the priesthood, who had evinced a rare discernment in the selection of boys encouraged to continue their studies, and who reported that from thirty-four boys sent from his parish to the diocesan college the total result was one priest.

The discussion had grown in interest. Some of us pursued it to the extent of going over the diocesan lists, the figures in which revealed that over eighty per cent of our clergy come from parishes distinctly rural, although two-thirds of the Catholic population are located in cities and towns. The rector of the diocesan seminary was next consulted. He stated that three-fourths of the students in actual attendance had grown up on the farm. Some of the priests interested in the inquiry enjoyed a familiar acquaintance with conditions in two other dioceses the titular cities of which have a Catholic population of about 50,000 and 250,000 respectively. The former of these has furnished thirteen of the present diocesan clergy, the latter sixty. In this investigation no effort was made to ascertain the birthplace; each priest was accredited to the parish in which his family resided at the time of his entering college. The highest result, therefore, these two cities can claim, is one priest from every four thousand Catholics; each nine hundred families furnishes one recruit to the ministry.

Since that time, with the aid of the Ecclesiastical Directory and census publications, we have endeavored to learn in what proportion city and country parishes in the United States are respectively contributing to the staffs of diocesan clergy. No account has been taken of the regular clergy, whose location in a diocese gives no clue, of course, to their place of birth or training. Paper information is at best second-class authority. The state-

RECRUITING OUR CLERGY

ments we venture to make with the information at our disposal any reader can revise with accuracy, at least as far as his own diocese is concerned. The inquiry did not extend to the newer or scattered dioceses of the West and South, conditions there up to the present time having been such as to preclude the possibility of recruiting a native clergy. The line of division aims at separating rural districts and smaller towns from larger towns and cities. In some cases it was impossible to ascertain the exact population of towns under consideration, and we agreed to class all towns having two or more parishes with the larger.

The following tables record the result:

| | | NUMBER OF PARISHES ||
NAME OF DIOCESE	CATHOLIC POPULATION FURNISHING ONE DIOCESAN PRIEST	IN CITIES AND LARGER TOWNS	IN SMALLER TOWNS AND COUNTRY PLACES
Baltimore	1,370	84	60
Boston	1,600	166	82
Chicago	2,000	273	58
Cincinnati	875	90	91
Dubuque	460	22	150
Milwaukee	830	110	114
New York	1,700	238	74
Philadelphia	1,250	197	82
St. Louis	1,300	107	134
St. Paul	900	73	133
Albany	1,000	73	63
Alton	550	33	84
Altoona	1,270	40	47
Belleville	550	19	81
Brooklyn	1,450	140	75
Buffalo	1,140	107	83
Burlington	950	18	86
Cleveland	1,380	130	54
Columbus	870	38	58

SOME PASTOR'S PROBLEMS

NAME OF DIOCESE	CATHOLIC POPULATION FUURNISHING ONE DIOCESAN PRIEST	NUMBER OF PARISHES IN CITIES AND LARGER TOWNS	TOWNS AND IN SMALLER COUNTRY PLACES
Covington	880	22	38
Davenport	450	29	63
Des Moines	480	12	45
Detroit	1,540	72	98
Erie	900	40	66
Fall River	1,260	59	15
Fort Wayne	720	62	68
Grand Rapids	1,060	52	56
Green Bay	860	45	111
Harrisburg	900	38	41
Hartford	1,450	110	85
Indianapolis	790	41	101
Kansas City	830	37	39
Leavenworth	690	29	64
La Crosse	690	31	113
Louisville	880	48	61
Manchester	1,025	34	43
Newark	1,600	140	57
Ogdensburg	750	15	78
Omaha	550	27	83
Peoria	640	66	90
Pittsburgh	1,300	188	107
Portland	1,050	24	57
Providence	1,350	64	29
Richmond	720	16	21
Rochester	800	52	57
Rockford	530	24	48
St. Cloud	700	16	81
St. Joseph	640	15	38
Scranton	1,060	80	95
Sioux City	500	22	83
Springfield	1,000	87	93
Syracuse	1,080	52	41
Toledo	930	37	56
Trenton	940	63	71
Wheeling	700	17	48
Wilmington	1,000	11	19
Winona	530	10	71

RECRUITING OUR CLERGY

If we recognize the time-honored standard—one priest for a thousand souls—it will be observed that the supply decreases the greater the proportion of the city parishes. This holds, with few exceptions, throughout, the dearth being especially notable in dioceses whose Catholic population is overwhelmingly urban. Such are Chicago, New York, Boston, Newark, Philadelphia, Brooklyn. On the other hand, dioceses in Illinois, Iowa, Indiana, or Wisconsin, where country parishes predominate and the large city is almost unknown, approach the standard of a priest for every five hundred souls. Moreover most dioceses with large city populations have been regularly adopting candidates for the priesthood from abroad. The contrary obtains in Iowa, Wisconsin, etc.

In examining the other forces which contribute to providing the diocesan clergy, it is worthy of note that New York, Brooklyn, Boston, Baltimore, Philadelphia, Buffalo, Newark, have had for years their own preparatory colleges and ecclesiastical seminaries. It is interesting also to contrast, for example, Cleveland and Dubuque, which respectively enjoy the advantage of a college and seminary conducted by their own diocesan clergy. The contrast may also be instituted between Rochester and Philadelphia, or Rochester and Buffalo. Or we might examine Buffalo, provided with a seminary for generations, side by side with Erie, which has had neither a seminary nor preparatory college.

Or, if we are to believe that location, surroundings, climate, exert an influence in the matter, it might be well to compare Chicago with the other dioceses in Illinois, Harrisburg with Philadelphia, Wheeling with Pittsburgh, Columbus and Toledo with Cleveland.

CHAPTER XIII

Importance of Rural Parishes

UNWARRANTED DIFFIDENCE

HOWEVER much contributors may differ about the extent to which Faith is imperiled by residence in a large city, no one regrets the presence of large numbers of our Catholic people in country parishes. The protection afforded there is manifest. That the city has dangers for many, if not for all, is undisputed. True, sixty years ago, so great a prelate as the late Archbishop Hughes for a time resisted the advocacy of locating Catholic immigrants on the land. But the experience of two generations since has so thoroughly taught another lesson, that it is doubtful if even one among our hierarchy would not enter enthusiastically into any project looking to the enlargement of the rural population at the sacrifice of members in the city parishes.

But while this community of sentiment prevails in reference to the general aspect of the question, there lurks in the minds of many of our clergy a certain diffidence of accomplishing anything by efforts in that direction. "You cannot resist the most vigorous tendency of the hour," is the common reply. "We are living in an age," they say, "where great masses of the population from all

RURAL PARISHES

classes and in every district gravitate toward large cities; there are a thousand reasons for their doing so; almost every consideration leads them there. It is inevitable that Catholics will go with the tide."

All this is too true. But, before resigning ourselves to the inevitable approach of a great evil, might not it be well to ask: "Have we tried?" Is every attempt to be dismissed as futile? If there is one thing more than another to be conceded, if there is one great fact which all must recognize, it is the little or no attention we have given to remedying a condition, the existence of which all are disposed to consider regrettable. Millions after millions of the most devoted Catholics that Europe has seen, came here in their helplessness. We made heroic efforts to give them opportunities of practising their Faith amid the dangers of our great cities; only rarely has anything been done to place them where those dangers did not obtain. Had a modicum of the effort and outlay required to establish and maintain parish schools for constant accessions of poor immigrants been expended on locating them in groups upon the land, no one to-day would look back upon the venture with anything but feelings of the deepest satisfaction. Had anyone a hundred years ago dared to promise that our parish school system, in spite of all the difficulties to be encountered, would eventually assume the proportions we witness in its attainments to-day, he should certainly have been regarded as a misguided visionary. Are a people and a clergy with such a record to faint in presence of this other great undertaking, an undertaking which is constantly revealing itself as one of the great works of zeal in the not too distant future?

SOME PASTOR'S PROBLEMS

What wonderful organizations may soon come into existence inspired by the purpose of acquiring land for the children of the Faith, only the prophet can at this stage depict. Meanwhile, the modest efforts of certain pastors and religious societies have accomplished much already.

INFLUENCES ACCOUNTABLE FOR THE DEPLETION OF COUNTRY DISTRICTS

Generally speaking, Catholics in relation to this endeavor may be classed under three heads—city residents in America, country residents in America, and immigrants from the old world. Until our social fabric undergoes some very extraordinary upheaval, we may as well set the first of these outside our calculations altogether. The young man of city rearing who will reconcile himself to country occupations and country habits of life is so decidedly exceptional as to be quite excluded from our plans. Of all in the past who reached maturity in the city, the number who voluntarily submitted to country life under any circumstances is not far removed from a minus quantity.

Of the second class, our American farm population, the great majority are contented with their lot, and would stay where they are. But ten thousand external influences have been at work to turn them from their present calling and scarcely one to continue them in it. Many intrinsic causes also contribute, such as higher wages, ligher work or shorter hours, places of amusement, etc. Even these would prove ineffective, did not the moral forces with which they come in contact operate in bringing about the same result.

RURAL PARISHES

The school system of the country is aimed directly at this. It has been the boast of legislators and supervisors of educational interests that the program of primary schools was framed to conduct pupils by the most direct route to the high school, and similarly, that every subject prescribed for high school work looked primarily to the students' future in the university or in some learned profession. It has been in every way to the interest of both primary and secondary school teachers to have the number entering a more advanced institution as large as possible. Their influence has been altogether in the direction of keeping the boy or girl at school, and by consequence, taking them from the farm. It is very flattering to the good father and mother to hear from the teacher, "Your boy is doing particularly well; his ability is much above the average; it is too bad not to give him a chance." Consequently, though very much needed at home they try to keep him at school, and one more is taken away from the prospect of being a country resident. What the regularly established schools of the State fail to accomplish, something called "business colleges," hanging out a sign in every little town, contrive to effect.

Everyone in the neighborhood whose opinion both child and parents are disposed to respect, commends the course and commends it highly. The local clergyman, physician, attorney, banker, editor, politician and other distinguished visitors to the home all agree in this. With nothing very definite in their promises, they spoke to the boy of a brilliant future, and praised parents who made such noble efforts to advance the future of their

SOME PASTOR'S PROBLEMS

family. The atmosphere of the high school was charged with this sentiment and with none other. The press of the land, public platforms, pulpits and similar oracles referred with pride to the large numbers our school system was advancing in the *higher walks of life*. The family were convinced beyond a shadow of doubt that wisdom lay in aspiring to professional and business careers and abandoning the more menial and less promising future that a rural district could provide.

Now, do we ever stop to reflect what would have been the issue if all this glorious array of forces had been faced in the opposite direction? What would have happened if schools, teachers, clergy, physicians, editors, etc.—throughout the land energized every conceivable effort in the endeavor to keep the young people of rural districts upon the farm? Are we quite sure that the cause of civil government, and civil society, would have been jeopardized?

OUR CONTRIBUTION TO THESE INFLUENCES

While all this was going on, where were we? On what side were we throwing our weight? Have there been any more ardent supporters of the "make something of yourself" cry than we? Have we not actually boasted over and over again, in public and private pronouncements, that we were *foremost* in every phase of this movement?

Our clergy everywhere encourage boys and girls to continue at school, altogether regardless of the consideration that continuing at school generally means continuing on the way to an avocation the following up of which is not possible in country dis-

RURAL PARISHES

tricts, regardless also of the further consideration that a growing interest in higher studies is usually accompanied by a declining interest in occupations and ambitions which attend life on the farm. The multiplication of Catholic colleges, by their very existence, not to speak of their conscious, intentional efforts in that direction, stands out before parents in rural surroundings as a recommendation of the great advantages such institutions are supposed to offer. Editors of Catholic weeklies seem to live in constant dread of the charge of unprogressiveness, did they not put forth their best efforts in urging higher education for the greatest possible number everywhere. Just previous to school opening this year an editorial in an influential Catholic paper began with these words "Schools open next week; every Catholic high school and college in the land should be filled to the utmost capacity." Have we an organ in the English-speaking world persistently daring to have no part in those clamors for the extension of higher education at the inevitable price of rural populations being depleted? A few years ago the Catholic representative of an Irish constituency told the British House of Commons that he cared little for this much-lauded commodity which they presumed to call "education," recognizing, as he did, that there was something of infinitely greater importance. True, such a remark coming from one of his attainments shocked this twentieth-century world. Yet would it not be wholesome to hear sometimes our Catholic editors announce the plain truth, that much of this uncompromising advocacy of learning and the incessant urging upon everyone to become a scholar is merely the worship of a fetish; or that much of the present-day enthusiasm for erecting, maintaining, patronizing great educational institutions is a poor substitute for satisfying the one worthy object of human aspiration, and that we who recognize the one thing necessary feel under no obligation to imitate their blind though strenuous ambitions; that, consequently, preserving a peasant population, though more or less illiterate, in the simple exercise of true Faith is an object much more to be sought after than providing increasing numbers with intellectual endowments?

MEANS OF PREVENTING THE DEPLETION

Now, let us suppose what would be the result if the entire force of the Catholic Church in America, throughout the different means at its disposal, were contributing to the cause of keeping Catholics in the country—contributing just to the extent to which such a condition is desirable, no further. Or rather, before abondoning the idea altogether, would it not be well to inquire if it is really so that the forces of Catholicity in our midst are hopelessly and absolutely without weight in this matter; if there is no person or no source of influence among us capable of guiding in an issue upon which the eternal salvation of many souls so largely depends?

In the first place, what about the rural pastor? Does anyone suppose that a priest so situated, convinced of the importance of this work, enjoying the confidence of his people, with all the opportunities at his disposal, in the pulpit, in the school or home, could fail, in the course of twenty, ten or even five years to be instrumental in restraining many—both old and young—who otherwise would

RURAL PARISHES

have yielded to the allurements and the thousand circumstances helping on this perpetual drift cityward? Then, there is the Mission, which in our day reaches every parish, and from which so many wholesome, consoling results are everywhere reported. If it were the practice of missionaries in each parish to devote one entire conference to this subject, should we not expect the faithful during those days, when they come to understand how trival are all worldly interests and attachments when weighed in the balance against an eternal kingdom on the one hand and eternal suffering on the other, would stand in horror of any fascination calculated to endanger their own or their children's future, and willingly reconcile themselves to the less inviting conditions attending their present situation? The more we think of this the more we should be astonished that missionary bands have up to the present paid so little attention to what everyone within or without the Church considers the growing evil of our day.

What of our Catholic schools? Their number in rural districts is constantly on the increase. We are proud of their efficiency, of the results they give. We know there are many pupils completing their early studies there who give a good account of themselves in schools and institutions more advanced. This is what we hear everywhere and unintermittingly. We have every reason to hope, therefore, that schools and teachers capable of such results could exert an untold influence, were their attention turned to pointing out, in season and out of season, how much the interest of immortal souls is safeguarded by continuing in the country far removed from the vanity and world-

SOME PASTOR'S PROBLEMS

liness, the frivolity and distraction, the pleasure-seeking and dissipation, the temptations and sins, so easily to be met with in large cities. With the young children of the land growing up in this condition, accepting such teaching in much the same spirit as they accept unceasing warnings against the dangers of public schools, mixed marriages, secret societies, the liquor traffic, etc.—their after-lives would, no doubt, be governed by an equal regard for all early impressions so received. I have never heard of a parish school attempting to exert influence in this direction even in the slightest degree. I know of many that are constantly holding out to their pupils a brilliant future in the learned professions or business careers. So long as we allow this attitude of mind to prevail in our primary institutions, we are hardly justified in pleading the impossibility of doing anything to keep Catholic people in the country. We might go on trying to conceive the possibilities of our position, did our colleges, academies and seminaries unite in this propaganda. The supposition that any such action could be hoped for may be visionary in the extreme; the outcome, should such action ever become a reality, no one will consider even doubtful.

Nowhere do Catholic papers find readers so devoted and faithful as in rural Catholic homes. Here the spirit of criticism is almost unknown. This weekly visitor is given lengthy entertainment; its statements are accepted without question, and in the families of long-term subscribers there are few, old or young, who do not sooner or later drink in its words. Sometimes when I read in the columns of these journals reiterated appeals for the support of the Catholic press, I wonder if their

RURAL PARISHES

editors realize how many faithful disciples they have in that portion of the population from whom least is heard. Now, urging claims of country life, advising its residents to be contented with their state, supporting the wishes of parents who endeavor to have their children remain there, gathering arguments, incidents, statistics from every available source that will have the effect of driving home those convictions more thoroughly, make up a form of literature altogether in keeping with the aims of a Catholic paper. Week after week their pages decry the public school; they teem with warnings against the demoralizing tendency of theatres and gambling rooms, the irreligious and often licentious atmosphere of what is called "society," the ever-increasing force of Socialism, the outward trend of divorce; they see with certainty that many children of the Church will be carried away in the tide. But they seem to forget that one large section of her children are practically immune to all those dangers, and that, consequently, the most effective means of protecting still greater numbers can be found in maintaining as many of the faithful as possible amid conditions which more than all others guarantee that immunity. What country parish in America is threatened with demoralization from the influences of mixed marriage, divorce, and socialism, or even from the more insidious influences of worldliness, pleasure-seeking, and dissipation? Why then throw up our hands in despair? Why exclaim that all efforts to keep our people in the country must necessarily prove futile, when we have not, up to the present, requisitioned to the task so powerful an engine as the Catholic press.

SOME PASTOR'S PROBLEMS

FINANCING THE IMMIGRANT

The other possibility—that of settling Catholic immigrants on the land—is a great work, scarcely begun yet. Undertakings so complex require time and organization. Failures in the past should give no cause for discouragement: they are merely necessary steps in a necessary experience. When we hear what has been accomplished in the Argentine or even in some parts of Western Canada, we begin to realize what the outlook is nearer home. We can picture a future in which hundreds of thousands of Europeans, adapted to farming occupations from youth, will be able to carry on in North America the occupations in which their parents and grandparents for generations gave such splendid examples of persevering Faith. Soon this may be the Church's greatest work of zeal on this side of the Atlantic. Immense sums of money, it is true, would be necessary to float a scheme whose dimensions have still to be calculated. Our wealthier Catholics come to understand that colleges, academies and schools have a claim on their surpluses and some have responded generously. Would not the gifts enabling Catholic immigrants to get a start on a farm advance the cause of Christ and Holy Church in an even more desirable way?

CHAPTER XIV

LANGUAGES IN PREPARATORY SEMINARIES

THE question whether or not the course of studies that we have followed with little deviation for generations gives the best possible results under present conditions, has been discussed at educational conventions of late, and answered in various ways. It will not be amiss to offer some further suggestions.

It may be presumed at the outset that the purpose of a preparatory seminary is chiefly threefold: (1) to give the student at least the foundation of a liberal education; (2) to carry him through such branches as are necessary to the prosecution of his studies in philosophy and theology; (3) to carry on, as far as it is possible at that stage, the work of equipping him for the practical duties of the ministry. While the curriculum of the higher seminary is concerned almost exclusively with the technical studies required by his sacred calling, the years leading up to it are devoted to what we are wont to regard as general education. Even though we insist that in those early years the practical is secondary, that formation must dictate the character of the work to be pursued, we can surely agree upon the advisability of combining the two whenever possible, and thereby giving preference to any branch of study of real practical

SOME PASTOR'S PROBLEMS

value, provided it can be used with equal force as an instrument of intellectual development.

Suppose we take one more look at the time-honored place of college studies from this point of view. At no time in history has the Church of any country been face to face with the problems which confront us in America and which arise from the multiplicity of languages spoken by the faithful here. There are pastors in this country who, in order to provide for the spiritual wants of all the people within the limits of a single parish, would need to hear confessions in fourteen or fifteen different tongues. The impossibility of meeting the situation must mean incalculable loss to the cause of God and immortal souls.

Then it must be remembered that many thousands of those whom we call foreigners come here possessed of a simple, earnest faith and need only the opportunity to persevere in it with fervor. Very often this opportunity cannot be given them. Nor was it always necessary that they should be given priests of deep and varied learning, of business capacity, of tact, of vigorous influence; any priest in good standing speaking their language could easily be instrumental in saving hundreds from error or negligence. From the point of view of tangible results is there anything in the program of preparatory seminaries deserving more urgent attention than this? The time which a college boy has been required to spend on Greek alone should suffice to give him a highly serviceable acquaintance with at least two modern languages.

Allow me to say in passing that there seems to be something radically wrong from the outstart in our method of teaching the modern living lan-

PREPARATORY STUDIES

guages. The case is almost unknown of a pupil learning to speak a language in one of our colleges. We accept this condition as inevitable. There are schools everywhere pursuing different systems in this line of endeavor and giving results in one-fourth the time we devote to these branches. Students of average ability in our colleges, many of them of more than average ability, attend classes in French or German three, four or five years, and at the end not only make no pretence of speaking the language, but never dream of attempting a letter to a French or German friend, nor imagine they should read a French or German newspaper with facility. To get through a certain number of grammar exercise and *translate* a page or perhaps a paragraph or two for each successive class usually measures the extent of their achievement. A straight case of failure to accomplish because of failure to attempt.

Unpardonably radical as it may seem, I shall dare propose doing away with Greek in order to give place for the study of such foreign languages as would be of practical service in the ministry. Hundreds, thousands of our clergy have distinct recollections of a laborious if not distasteful and uninteresting apprenticeship struggling with τυπτω or λυω, or Homeric dialects. What benefit from it all? In what way does it serve them in afterlife? The treasures awaiting them, stored up in the richest literature civilization has known, they never reach, of course. How many priests ever open a Greek author after Rhetoric year? Now and then we meet one who does and he is usually in the same class with the one we remember to have conjugated the three voices of λυω without a halt and had all

SOME PASTOR'S PROBLEMS

the exceptions in the third declension on the tip of his tongue: they both go through life bookworms.

Why continue this intolerable farce in our college work? "Oh," someone may say, "this is the method of drill which makes a man, gives him steadiness of habits, tries his patience, stimulates determination, makes him industrious, improves his memory," etc., etc. Very true; but could not all these results be obtained in the acquisition of Polish, or Hungarian, or Rumanian? Does a language cease to have an educative value just because it will be useful in after life? Or does the farm-boy's race after the cows not develop his muscles as surely as the time spent on a quartermile track in the gymnasium?

Again, it is argued that Catholic institutions must continue the study of Greek because of the service it renders to the study of Sacred Scripture. In this respect it is of equal importance with Hebrew and Syro-Chaldaic and is entitled to the same attention. There will always be a goodly number looking to university degrees, post-graduate courses, and a life of study, to whom we may safely entrust both the interpretation and preservation of the original and traditional publications of the Sacred Text.

"But," says your professor who has learned to love Homeric metres and is quite sure that Plato's philosophical tenets are understood only in the original, "we could not think of leaving out Greek; you know we have always had it." Precisely; sentiment must have its place. Do not ask us to be guided by results. Just let us continue in the blissful enjoyment of the past. Seriously, I should liké to ask our professor friend is there not always a danger of imposing upon the pupils the very subjects in which we are personally interested, altogether forgetful of

PREPARATORY STUDIES

what it is that the pupil really needs. In one university of my acquaintance the president was a classical scholar and for some years had made a specialty of Latin and Greek epigraphy. Soon after his appointment epigraphy became a compulsory subject in the department of classics. His successor, who was at the same time professor of History, was writing books on archeology. Very soon epigraphy disappeared from the curriculum; but thereafter students who wished to make a special study of History found nearly all their time given over to archeology and ethnology. And with similar instincts the Catholic professor of classics is disposed to argue that Greek was on the curriculum of colleges everywhere years before he was born; that the most learned men we have ever known were Greek scholars, and we ourselves enjoy Greek immensely—why then ask us to consider the results which all this yields? Why distract us in our blissful and peaceful state?

Are we having adequate return for the time spent on Latin? Ordinarily it may be maintained that the seminarian who can use his text books in philosophy and theology to advantage and follow his class work during those six years has a familiarity with Latin quite sufficient for all the practical purposes of afterlife. When the preparatory institution has given him the capacity to read his seminary text books readily, its duty toward this branch of study may be considered fulfilled. Experience has taught us that in many cases something less is the actual result. When it is remembered that more than one-fourth of the time for six long years of a college course is given to Latin, one is tempted to suggest that there must be something visionary in the aspirations which

SOME PASTOR'S PROBLEMS

govern the method of dealing with it. Why not abandon forever the hope that parish priests and assistants of the twentieth century will pass their leisure hours luxuriating in the literary beauties of Livy and Horace? If such has obtained anywhere or at any time in the past, what has been the profit to the interests of Holy Church? Should any of our clergy have time or inclination for Latin literature, why should it be absorbed in familiarizing themselves with the revelings of pagan authors? Few of us who are giving our lives to college duties can easily escape the rebuke which the late Canon Sheehan puts in the mouth of Geoffrey Austin. Looking back over life, his keen regret was not to have been introduced in college to the works of the Christian writers, to the exclusion, at least in part, of the literature of ancient Greece and Rome.

Every year and every week we spend a large proportion of our time teaching the class to write Latin prose. A certain amount of this is strictly necessary, especially in earlier years. Without that rather thorough drill provided for in more elementary text books, many students would not acquire due familiarity with the details of Latin syntax and idiom. No one could propose neglecting this. But of what value are all those exercises in Latin composition adhered to so scrupulously until the very last hour of a classical course? How much has your ecclesiastical student gained in any respect by those themes two or three or four times weekly? What power do they give him? What culture do they give him? You say he learns to write Latin —and if so, what of it? What use does a priest make of this accomplishment? One in twenty may be called upon to write a Latin letter or a Latin

PREPARATORY STUDIES

document at rare intervals; one in a thousand must do so frequently; and to provide for such contingencies every student in a preparatory college or seminary must squander, perhaps one-fourth or one-fifth of his time for five or six years. As a matter of fact those priests who have acquired a facility in writing or speaking Latin owe it not to paragraphs worked out in imitation of passages from Cicero or Livy, but to the classes in philosophy and theology in which Latin was the language spoken. It is very important that the ecclesiastical student should read Latin readily at the end of his preparatory course. Reading power is the object to be attained in a Latin course; let us understand this definitely; ability to read Latin, not ability to write it, is what will be of practical value, and this object is served but very feebly by an unending round of such exercises in Latin prose composition.

It will be contended, perhaps, that writing Latin should continue to receive a great deal of attention because of the mental culture acquired thereby. Are we quite sure of this? What form of culture does this training impart? It calls for very little exercise of the reasoning faculties. Many a student stands first in a Latin composition test who could never in a lifetime grasp Euclid's demonstration of the truth that "the angles at the base of an isosceles triangle are equal to one another." Many a student has carried off the prize in Latin composition who lacked reasoning power sufficient to follow the argument in Cicero's *Pro Milone*. Writing a presentable Latin paragraph or essay does not call for any intellectual effort; it is, in the main, a matter of memory and imitation. What type of character does such a training develop? A man who never thinks for himself, because he has become habituated to letting others do that, his function being to do as they do and say, is just the product to be expected from a course of six or eight years in which memory and imitation exercises are the dominant element. Wherever that spirit has prevailed among what are considered the educated and cultured classes, where movements have become possible upon one or two raising a cry and enlisting the support of an unquestioning multitude, all the rest being willing to adopt a given course because their leader is willing, we shall generally find that the so-called education and culture have been acquired in the daily prosecution of tasks calling for no effort beyond what was possible through a good memory and a capacity for imitation. There are many who never think for themselves, because their college course was filled up with Latin prose exercises and mental pabula of that description. If we would turn out men of deliberate conviction, men who stand on principal because they are capable of grasping principles, men who would examine a case on its merits and be governed accordingly in their sympathies and in their support, men who will be above personal considerations and local prejudices and racial animosities, men who can be reasoned with, let us have a program of studies that call for an exercise of reason.

I have known children who spoke both French and English before commencing school, before the age at which it is ordinarily supposed we attain to the use of reason. No doubt in the days of Cicero, many children of six or seven years spoke both Latin and Greek with equal readiness. Are we to give

PREPARATORY STUDIES

seven or eight years in college to acquiring a facility which under other conditions children are in possession of before reaching the age of primary school entrance. I have met half-breeds in Western Canada who spoke English, French and Indian, all three without the least difficulty. They had never gone to school, but certainly with ordinary opportunities might have learned to read and write all three before the age of fourteen or fifteen. Moreover, this could be accomplished by minds incapable of making any progress in algebra or logic. What would have hindered those people, *mutatis mutandis,* from reading and writing Latin with perfect ease at the age of fifteen? And this is more than we accomplish in eight years of Latin prose composition.

Before passing to another topic I should like to propose the following subject for debate: "Resolved that the time spent upon Latin and Greek in our preparatory institutions deprives their students of literary training." Our curriculum does little or nothing to familiarize them with, to arouse their interest in, to give them a taste for solid reading in their native tongue. It may be interposed in retort that a priest's life should not permit much time for such occupation. No one doubts, however, that from every point of view, practical or otherwise, a certain amount of solid reading is commendable and no one fails to see the desirability of so occupying some of the time which otherwise would be given to newspapers and magazines. Is not the first purpose of an education to elevate the student's taste in this direction, to familiarize him step by step with the best specimens that the language affords, and thus to make use of the most direct means to give him a lasting interest in works of this kind? That for a number of years his studies should have been serious, though confined to other departments of learning, will not guarantee his attachment to the more serious works in English literature. On the contrary, that he has been made to scorn delights and live laborious days amid his Latin and Greek text books will not of itself arouse a keen interest in any other form of literature. As an exemplification of this, how few priests from the Atlantic to the Pacific read Newman or Brownson, notwithstanding their ten or twelve years of drill in studies requiring effort and application. Does this reflect upon their teachers? Why do they not read them? Clearly *because they were not brought up to read them.* If Newman and Brownson had been given a place in the curriculum on an equal footing with Cicero, Cæsar, and Homer, would not the result be different? If some of the hours upon hours and days upon days and years upon years in which we thumbed over Latin dictionaries, and memorized rules of euphony, and tried to recite endless exceptions to the rules for gender, and railed against the tediousness of Latin prosody and the increments in *a, i,* and *o,* had been devoted not to a mere cursory reading, but to a real serious study under a teacher's guidance, of those great classics penned by Catholic authors, going through them section by section, and paragraph by paragraph with all the thoroughness we were made bring to bear upon the assigned thirty lines of Livy or Homer, does anyone doubt that Newman and Brownson would be intimate companions of many a pastor for the remainder of his days? There are laymen, lay Catholics, generally converts, who have never had the advantage of a college education and

PREPARATORY STUDIES

who are constant readers of just such works as these, not because they are better students than it is our privilege to form, not because they are more highly gifted intellectually, but simply because some circumstance in earlier life or some associates turned their attention to these works. There is yet much to improve in the course of English literature attempted by our colleges and preparatory seminaries.

Old text books were a unit in defining English Grammar as "The art of speaking and writing the English language correctly," though in reality many a one has done both without giving any time to grammar studies. If nothing more than avoiding grammatical mistakes were accomplished in the study of grammar, a few weeks' course, sufficient to point out all the difficulties, would complete this portion of a school program. The business world and social world afford many examples of people whose conversation and correspondence satisfy all the requirements of the strictest syntax; several of these nevertheless never belonged to a class in grammar. The proper handling of this important branch of study undertakes something much higher and much more difficult. It is altogether an analytic process. Its exercises have to do not with the forms and inflections of words, but with the intricacies of thought which through their relations and correlations these words express. To analyze or parse implies essentially an understanding of the meaning of the sentence, a thorough grasp of the thought which lies beneath it. Students who have been drilled for years in the grammatical analysis of sentences usually prove capable of occupying themselves with what is abstruse

SOME PASTOR'S PROBLEMS

and subtle and are thus best prepared to enter upon the reading of literary treatises which are learned and profound.

On the other hand nothing so marks the enervating tendency of present-day school work as the disposition to minimize the importance of grammatical analysis. As Cardinal Newman says, "The student who proclaims his dislike for the study of grammar has found another way of saying that he does not like work." This is one branch of study in which there is no royal road to success. Application alone brings results and the college boy who gains results without it has indisputable evidence that his career is other than one in which education is a requisite. Admitting that a logical mind is the final test of mental development, the *summum bonum* of the true scholar, we shall not fail to recognize that among all the branches of earlier study the one which most surely trains to logical accuracy is the grammar study of our own English language.

One further consideration here relative to the teaching of English. There are many congregations in the land which are present at the reading of the Epistle and Holy Gospel Sunday after Sunday and hear them not. It is not because the church is large or the reader's voice too weak. Nor is it lack of good disposition on the part of the flock. There is reading which commands the attention of an audience and reading which commands it not. The latter is far from uncommon. Is it not quite possible that an accomplishment often acquired in the home circle by a child of twelve or fourteen should be in the possession of any boy at the end of six years in a preparatory seminary or college? Surely he whose profession will impose the lifelong task of public

PREPARATORY STUDIES

speaking cannot commence the preparation too soon, at least the preparation to make himself heard.

The writer does not pretend that there is any justification whatever for speaking of Christian doctrine last of all. We are to assume that every student looking to the priesthood knows his Catechism. Is there any reason why every student in preparatory seminaries should not have the training required for a catechist? Is there a priest anywhere who is negligent in this awfully important duty? If there be one for whom the task is irksome and tedious, may it not be contended that this deplorable condition of things is due to one or other of two causes—the want of necessary training in the art of catechizing, or having begun the exercises of this art too late in life? To say that a priest has no love for the work of religious instruction is to say that the vocation we received from God has no attractiveness for us. A zealous interest in the religious training of young children is absolutely inseparable from a sacerdotal vocation. But like every other gift or sentiment associated with that sacred calling it may develop and increase, or disappear and be lost. No care is too great to bestow on the aspirant to the ministry, even during his early college years, that his interest in teaching Catechism may be aroused and permanently sustained. If the Church is preëminently a teaching institution, the colleges which prepare candidates for the ministry are preëminently formers of teachers. Of our ability to realize this view it might be said that "the children of this world are wiser in their generation than the children of light." Secular normal schools produce real secular teachers. Do we produce successful religious teachers? Out of a class of one hundred having the advantage of

SOME PASTOR'S PROBLEMS

one year in a normal school ninety will do satisfactory work the first year of their engagement. Many of these have no special natural aptitude for the work; they are not looking to it as a lifetime occupation. Nevertheless a systematic training during that one normal school year does really fit them for the task. Why would not our Catholic colleges undertake to give every student within their walls a similar training for handling a Catechism class? Why would not every student within the wall of a preparatory college or seminary be turned out an expert in the art of teaching Christian doctrine?

THE END